Sterling Script

A Local Author Collection
2018

Walper Publishing
Sterling Heights, Michigan

Editors
Tuesday Morning Writers
Rena Davis, Katy Hojnacki, Terry Hojnacki,
Cynthia Anne Hurt, and Rebecca Eve Schweitzer

Editor-in-Chief
Terry Hojnacki

Cover Art & Design
Katy Hojnacki

All rights reserved.
Copyright 2018 Walper Publishing
Printed in the United States of America

ISBN: 978-1-949224-00-9
Library of Congress Control Number: 2018946381

Reference photography provided by: *Cynthia Anne Hurt*

The selections printed in this collection reflect the authors'
original work as submitted to the
Local Author Collection.

First Edition
1 2 3 4 5 6 7 8 9 10

Many thanks
to all the authors and editors
in our vibrant writing community
for making this project possible.

Happy Writing

TABLE of CONTENTS

Dear Reader,

Our mission is to support and encourage the local writing community by publishing their short stories, poetry, and creative nonfiction works. Whether you enjoy a fun-filled fantasy adventure, romantic poetry, or eerie tales, there is something for everyone in this collection.

As Nathaniel Hawthorne said, "Good reading is damn hard writing." Our authors have put in the hard work writing.

Happy Reading,

Terry

Broas Mann

Born and raised in Detroit, Michigan, Broas Mann obtained Mechanical Engineering degrees from Illinois Institute of Technology and Northwestern University. He was an instructor in that field at Lawrence Institute of Technology, after which he enjoyed fifty years as a Research Engineer and Consultant with Chrysler Corporation.

Mann and his wife have four children, eight grandchildren and eight great-grandchildren, and his primary interest is centered on these families. He also enjoys writing, and the study of genealogy.

From many years of research, and several visits to the town of Belding, Michigan, much of the available Broas family history was documented. Based on this information, he has published a semi-fictional three volume trilogy titled *The Journal of Levi Broas.*

FRED

Broas Mann

We knew him almost from the time he was born. Fred entered our world one spring day by falling (or being pushed?) from his nest in our Norway maple. His reaction to this beginning was prophetic: he crawled, stumbled and flopped into the open garage to rest behind the left rear wheel of the family car, disabling it for the day. Endless chirping, poking and cajoling by Fred, Sr. had no effect; he would not budge. Then nature, in the form of a big yellow tomcat creeping out of the nearest shrub, accomplished in seconds what hours of parental urging could not: little Fred soloed. Wings, feet and beak all churning, he rose majestically to an altitude of about three inches and skimmed out of the garage, over the drive, the lawn, the sidewalk and the street, almost to the other side. But, alas, the curbs in our neighborhood are *four* inches high.

Fortunately, the tomcat lost interest, or was a bit myopic and did not see Fred's inglorious fall to earth. He spent that evening in the gutter recuperating from the abrupt termination of his maiden flight.

We saw a lot of Fred and his family that summer; they were regulars in our garden and at the feeder. But his next clash with the structures of man occurred one September afternoon. We observed him motionless in the middle of the yard, thoroughly saturated by a driving rain. (Robins don't mind a little water, but they are not amphibious.) We suspected all was not well when we noticed his left wing protruding at an angle suitable only for hitchhiking.

We have a large sliding glass door at the back of the house in which the reflection of the yard must look, to a bird in flight, like the forest primeval—its victims have been legend. Fred did everything with abandon, and he must have hit that door at just under Mach 1, which would have accounted for his apparently deceased condition. He remained motionless for over an hour in the rain. Then the rain stopped—he still did not move. Finally the kids decided he deserved a decent burial and were in the midst of putting together some kind of avian funeral ritual when one eye opened, then the other. The memorial service became an intense vigil as all attention was riveted on Fred's recovery. After another hour he managed to get himself right side up, but he wasn't about to fly. He was still dazed and his left wing still resembled a brakeman's flag.

Just then Nature took another of her inexplicable turns. The same yellow tomcat that had missed a young-robin-lunch that spring poked his greedy snout from under the nearby hedge. He surveyed the scene carefully and then began that feline belly-crawl that had kept his ancestors—both wild and domesticated—well fed for centuries. When he was about eight feet away, he stopped and coiled his springs for the final leap. We watched in awe, wanting to help but somehow were hypnotized by this ancient ritual.

Young Sara, our resident humanitarian, broke the spell. She sprang at the same instant as the tom, deflected the hurtling bundle of claws and fur with one hand and scooped up Fred with the other. This second shock brought the bird out of his reverie and he thrashed about, trying to escape Sara's grasp.

Meanwhile, the cat recovered his senses enough to realize that he had once again been cheated out of a well-earned meal, and he resented it. While Sara held the struggling bird high overhead, the cat stalked round and round. He could probably have jumped as high as a 10 year old's hands can reach, but he was just a little leery of the human that had dared challenge a ferocious feline in mid-flight, and was even now screaming and kicking at him. Finally, Joan of Arc realized that Fred had recovered enough to take over his own defense; she eased her grasp and a badly ruffled robin launched himself headlong into the nearest tall bush, safe from the hungry tom, and spent the rest of the day alternately preening and shuddering.

Our last direct contact with Fred came just before Christmas of that year, and it demonstrates a known, but not often seen, relationship among the non-human members of the animal world. We had a small, scrawny, very lovable dog at that time—Soleil, a name that aptly fitted her disposition. Despite several ailments, including diabetes and the accompanying semi-blindness, her sole aim in the short time left to her was to please those creatures around her, especially the ones low enough and close enough for her to see. Now while a robin on the ground would fit the first of those conditions, you would hardly expect it to fit the second. But, as we may have demonstrated by now, Fred was no ordinary robin.

From previous contacts, and despite his earlier escapades with the tomcat, Fred knew that Soleil was the friendly type. Perhaps some avian sixth sense told him that canines are not felines. In any event, over the summer they had developed a tolerance for each other—recognizing that they shared the same backyard lawn, shrubbery and trees (although in this last case, for widely different reasons).

Gradually, however, tolerance grew into something more—they seemed almost to play a game of "catch me if you can," but without the deadly intent. You might wonder how a half-blind dog could play anything with a winged creature, but somehow Fred understood her limitation, for if

Soleil stood still, looking helplessly around her, he would fly back into her field of vision and the game would begin again.

Then Soleil made a fascinating discovery about robins: for some strange reason they collect those long wiggly red things that live in the ground. So it became another game for them—Soleil would scratch in the garden until part of a hapless worm was exposed—then she would back off and let Fred, who had been watching with avid interest, seize the disgusting thing by its head (or tail?), yank it all the way out, and fly out of sight with it. Of course, to Fred it was no game at all but an endless string of free lunches. However, as we all know, "there ain't no such thing" and Fred, being a first year rookie, never really learned to forage for himself.

The snows came early that year, and for a while, Soleil continued to play with Fred and to scrape away the white stuff, scratch the ground and find treats for him.

But her end was approaching, and by November she was too weak for any outdoor activities beyond her hygienic needs. All the years of love and care we had lavished on each other demanded that we end her suffering, so we had her put to sleep. As it turned out, this may also have been a death sentence for Fred, because during a Christmas week warm spell we found him under one of the shrubs where the worm supply had been plentiful, as long as Soleil was there to dig them out.

Perhaps they are once again playing "catch me if you can."

Nicole e. Castle

As a writer of dark poetry and short fiction, Nicole e. Castle is drawn to what lurks in the shadows. She has been published in the following: *Wayne Literary Review*, *Pink Panther Magazine*, *Erie Tales;* and *Between the Lines.*

Currently, she teaches composition and literature in southeastern Michigan, hosts a literary reading series called WORDcraft Wednesdays, and edits the college's literary magazine, *ARTIFEX.* She is also a proud member of the board for the Great Lakes Association of Horror Writers and editor of their horror short story/poetry magazine, *Ghostlight: The Magazine of Terror* and the mini-anthology, *Recurring Nightmares.*

Contact her at weirdnicolewrites@yahoo.com or *Weird Tale Author Nicole e. Castle* on Facebook.

one day my prince will come

Nicole e. Castle

loneliness is
being a god
riding a broken down carousel

Breath

Nicole e. Castle

—For Mr. Bradbury

The autumn people move into town

in a flurry of dead leaves

they slink along the whispers of hidden trysts,

> the sweat of a bully's closed fist,

> the pout of a child's swollen lip,

> the caravan sets up in the dead of night

> amidst dog whimpers, clutched sheets,

> night terrors

The carnival slumbers, dreaming, restless

> *Can you hear its deep, haggard breath?*

> *Feel its spittle on your brow, its hunger?*

reaching across fields, meadows, quiet

streets, into a house with a white picket fence,

roses, a porch swing

Come dawn, the sun bathes your lover in gold

you don't reach for him, instead you

leave the warm cocoon of your

bed,

and walk out the front door, past the porch swing,

the white picket fence, the thorn bush,

never looking back

with a flurry of dead leaves

at your feet.

Story Time,
or This Isn't Quite How I Remember It

Nicole e. Castle

Because of my mother's wants

And my father's stupidity

now I suffer.

She was a witch, for God's sake!

Out of the arms of my mother and into hers.

Now my home is this stony tower.

She thinks I love her as she sucks me dry.

Would she still want me if I was shorn?

      Pitiful.

Never am I more alone than when you come to me.

I don't know which I despise more—

her cold, bony fingers caressing my face, or your

hot, sweaty ones.

From one captor to another.

      Loathsome.

I am simply a possession to you.

You want nothing but this fleshy shell.

But what of my mind?

A mind that can see beyond these stone walls

and tiny window,

beyond the rolling green hills,

beyond woeful old women and bumbling young men,

where I can stand alone

with only the sun and the rain and my own raging tears.

I stand on this tiny window sill and I can almost reach the sun.

It sears my fingers, cradling me in its warmth.

I ignore the witch's screams.

I

am

free.

Carl Virgilio

Carl Virgilio is 70 years old and retired (since late 2008) from General Motors where he supervised the setup of product research clinics/focus groups nationwide.

He is single (divorced) and has two grown children, Matthew and Alyssa.

Virgilio has been writing (seriously/consistently) since his retirement from GM (anthology – poetry, prose, and short stories).

Dementia

Carl Virgilio

He glanced down to frail wrist, half covered by cuff,
unfamiliar – the dial, rebuffed now, enough,

the integers, 60, in Roman to 12,
2 long and 1 short – 3 sticks, what the hell!

Snuck candy into the dollar show,
Now Playing
Still Alice
back when…

My kids – their names, are they Matthew and Sally,
did I know, did I learn, how to bend?

The taste of milk chocolate, the first time ever.
Still Alice, just how did it end?

My kids – their names, are they Jeffrey and Aly,
just how will this cruel story end?

The taste of milk chocolate, the first time ever.
Still Alice, did I ask how it ends?

Was there laughter and joy, was love mentioned – forever,
was my other, my lover, my friend?

My kids, their names, they are Matt and my Aly!
The sun shines today, and did then

Isabel's place

Carl Virgilio

Isabel's place at the end of my street,
the sweet smells of licorice and pastry treats.

For me, penny candy, and a warm, friendly smile.
Her comfort, our time, street cornered exile.

Slipped through the cracks, this marked German Jew,
branded forever, 291462.

"Come back tomorrow, now promise me sweet,
half then for you, and the other for me."

"We'll talk of your future, and how happy you'll be,
half then for you, this fine pastry treat."

One day, just in passing,

STORE CLOSED

Family Death

discovered years later, her whispered last breath,

"Eli torn from me, my life's love, my young son,
I leave now to join him." 291461.

Take-A-Number

Carl Virgilio

Take-A-Number. Her number matched sequentially to the
first three of the six "burned" into her forearm.
Good morning, Mrs. Levine. And how are you today?

Just fine Mr. Schmidt, *and where were you that day?*

A glorious spring day, indeed! Would you not agree, Mrs.
Levine?

Yes, I would agree with you, it is a beautiful day *as I emerge,
still, from that harsh, arduous, life changing winter's day past, you son-
of-a-bitch. Were you the one, of a thousand and one; were you the one
with the dog? My newborn, ripped from me, was torn to shreds, the jaws
of Aryans' dog. But your intent, Mr. Schmidt was diminished; realize
that my newborn was breathless; my newborn was already dead. Your
line dog was German, a* **Shepherd**, *ironic this modern day stead.*

What can I do for you, Mrs. Levine?

Yes… please, Mr. Schmidt, two pounds of whitefish, four
cups of that *German style* potato salad, the corned beef – this

brisket over here, and two loaves, the black bread, *and a pound or two of your flesh Karl Schmidt.*

Will that be all, Mrs. Levine?

Yes, Mr. Schmidt. Have a wonderful day. *No! I have learned that you have been summoned, and are "entitled" to your day in court, due you through the democracy and the* **decency** *of this wonderful land that we now occupy, side by side. Soon. The third day, this May. I will be there as witness, focused on your cold and chiseled features, your deep blue and distant eyes, and your gray/wheat colored mane. Yes, Karl Schmidt, I will be there as witness to your probable,* **inevitable** *demise.*

And in kind, Mrs. Levine. Until we meet again.

A.F. Jerzowski

A.F. Jerzowski has been dabbling in creative writing for years. As a recent graduate of Oakland University with a concentration in writing and rhetoric, she has decided to pursue her dream.

Hoping to publish her first novel within the next year, Ann's dream may become reality. Not only does she want her novel out there, but also she wants to spread the message of "rescue" or "adopt, don't shop." This novel is based on a true story of a dog she adopted. The working title is: "Izzy's Story: The Mill and Beyond."

My Castle

A.F. Jerzowski

Scattered around a muddy field of written content, my words wander—grouping, attaching, forming, multiplying, sometimes stumbling over one another—meanings jumbled, misunderstood, working toward clarity.

Climbing the hill of dangling participles, I slide down the steep slope of run-on sentences and fall into a patch of points of view. Rolling around I/we, bumping into you/yours, then jumping up with the assistance of they/them, I move on.

Chopping through a copse of sentence fragments, I relish in a mild shower of adjectives, then break through a wall of quotes and take a deep sigh of relief. I find myself staring at the Castle of Clarity. I just need to run through a lovely field of adverbs and call for the bridge to be dropped over the moat of writer's block. Two short paragraphs later, I stand on one side of the moat, calling for the positioned end parenthesis to start the bridge lowering. Up on the wall of the castle, I notice that "end p" is staring at a turret. *He does not hear me,* I realize.

A beginning parenthesis taps on my shoulder and hands me a cell phone. "Text your request," she says.

End parenthesis looks at his phone, turns, waves, and drops the bridge. As I walk through the gates I am overwhelmed with the beauty of the castle. *How can it be imposing and welcoming at the same time?* I wonder, while deciding the creamy stone walls resemble my best linen card stock. I see writers sitting at small tables strategically placed around the courtyard. Ludicrous as it may seem, there are as many handwriting with pens and pencils as there are using laptops. *What century is this?*

Three large doors stare at me from across the courtyard. A man—wait, no, yes—my history teacher from high school, is pointing at the doors in order from left to right, door #1, door #2, door #3, inviting me to choose. *But I don't want to repeat the mistakes of the past.* I wave to Mr. History and turn to my right. A man is holding a scroll of typeset words. His smile reminds me of my journalism instructor, also from high school. He unfurls the roll of copy and it creates a path to a small alcove with "door #4" on it. As I walk along the side of the carpet of copy, I realize it is my original horoscope column from the school paper. I remember what fun it was to write all those years ago.

Deciding to trust what was behind door #4, I open it and step inside, shocked to walk into a huge, ornate bathroom. *A shower sounds great.* I shed years of regret, like soiled clothing, and flip them into a pile in a corner. My bare feet enjoy heated marble tiles. The Carpenters, "We've Only Just Begun," is playing softly. As I listen to my school song from my graduating class, I step into the shower. Crystal clear thoughts and ideas drop from the showerhead like warm rain dancing on a windowsill.

Refreshed and invigorated, I wrap myself in a fluffy robe of contentment and cozy slippers. A sense of familiarity comes over me as I walk down the hall into my kitchen—my regular kitchen from my real-life home. The delicious scent of brewing coffee greets me. Italian dark roast is dripping into a mug; a perfect hard-boiled egg is sitting in an eggcup; and, toast pops up from the toaster. Just as I pick up my adorable dog and he licks my chin, I look out the French doors leading from the breakfast nook to the front of the house and straight out the bow window in the dining room. A child is playing in a tall pile of leaves on my neighbor's lawn. A light source bounces off my right eye and I turn to see where it is originating. My old puppy is still in my arms as I spot the ornate silver-framed piece sitting on the granite countertop.

It is the only thing I don't recognize in my kitchen.

I move toward it, look closer, and read the inscribed words intricately woven into silver vines on the frame.

"Everything you need is right here," I read aloud, glancing at the mirror inside the frame. I am pictured there, holding my dog, a glimpse of the coffee maker on the counter to my right, a corner of the laptop on the breakfast table to my left.

Gently lowering my sweet, old dog to the floor, I get the egg, toast, and coffee, then sit down in front of the laptop. Freeing my hands of the food, I open the laptop to a new document.

The page is blank.

I smile as my fingers type.

Mark Morgan

Mark Morgan, Jr. is a Detroit native, teacher, and poet. A member of Detroit Writer's Guild, Mark enjoys meetings with the Poetry Workshop in Saint Clair Shores and the Creative Writers Workshop in Sterling Heights. His work has been published online by *The Rising Phoenix Review* and in print by *ARTIFEX*. Read more of Mark's poems on his blog, An Autumn Road, at anautumnroad.tumblr.com.

1000 eYeS

Mark Morgan

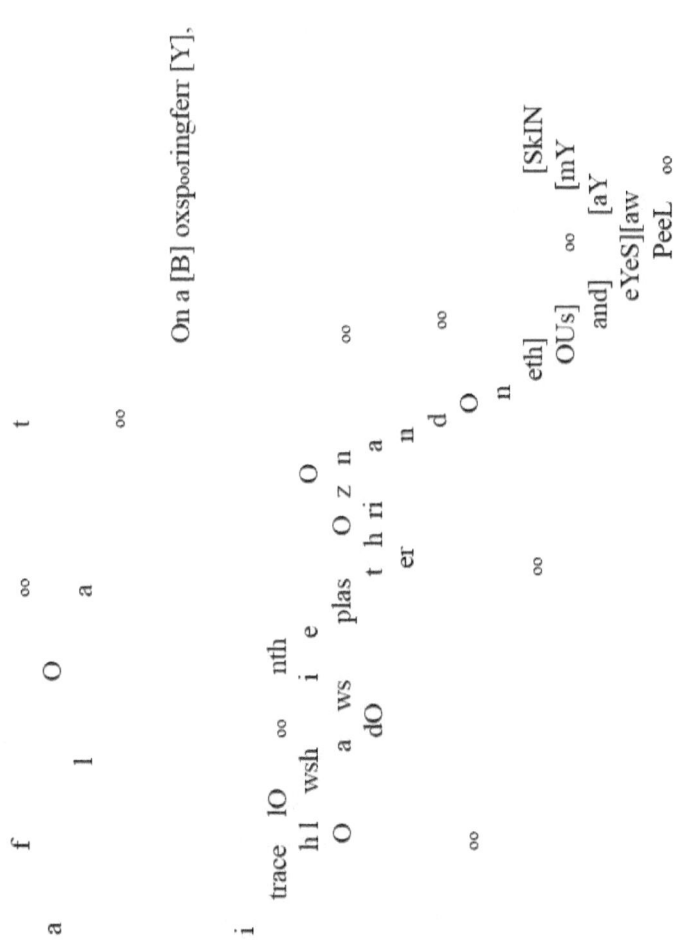

the other night

Mark Morgan

I watched streetlight specters crawl across my wall
and haunt the far corners of my room. exhaust
bled from an old Volkswagon's muffler and lit
    my lungs aflame with pure dusk

shut the window
I thought. but it was hot as hell outside and
I was used to fumes stinging my eyes. the bug
only comes by every few days anyhow
    when the air cleared, I smelled the

evening hear
again. my heart exploded from my rib cage,
crushing everything in fuzzy systolic
bear hugs before dragging my brain down dirt roads
    through firehoops and explosions
  heaving me up
  till I crash into stormclouds

        murmuring
           low

  in the sky
    in my temple
      in my throat
        dust
  kicked up the temperamental breeze
    mixed with rain, staining my face

with acid shame
the bare walls mocked with halfhearted echoes. shut
the window, I thought, because the last sunrise
you saw without a thousand mirrors ended
    long before the other night

Moonbeams

Mark Morgan

as apple blossoms splay their pinkened wings
against the sun's vehement burning rays
their feathers fall in sync with fleeting days
robins flood the sky like rubies and sing
joyous litanies. hoarded twigs and strings
crown the sunset, speckled turquoise ablaze
on blooming boughs that writhing winds will sway
and one day break—though sundered, dawn's blessings
are moonbeams bruised by spring rain, violets
tucking away the storm clouds in their cheeks,
fireflies smearing a waxed face with war paint—
silhouettes crackle like old frost. silence
melts beneath amethyst clouds as I strain
against gusts to hear midnight's beauty speak

Katy Hojnacki

Katy Hojnacki is a writer, artist, and avid gamer. She graduated from Oakland University with a degree in English and Studio Art.

She is an active member of the Sterling Heights Creative Writers Workshop as well as the Tuesday Morning Writers. Katy works with painting, novels, short stories, and even comics to delve into fantasy worlds.

Hide & Seek

Katy Hojnacki

"Come and play with us."

"Just one game."

"It'll be fun."

"Please, Adam, let's go." My sister turned to me with wide eyes. She held her hand out to help me out of bed.

"Nikki, no, just go back to sleep." I shushed my sister and shook my head.

The children outside kept tapping on the window. "Don't be a spoilsport. Come play."

"This is why no one plays with you at school, Adam. You're no fun," said Nikki, pouting.

I winced and took my sister's hand. She smiled and put a finger to her lips as we snuck across the sitting room to the front door. Outside the open window, I heard the others whispering excitedly.

The floor creaked under my bare feet. Nikki shot me a look. We both stared at the door to my parents' room. We listened for the groan of the bed frame. Someone could wake up and come to the door.

We waited for a light to click on, but it didn't. The cottage was silent.

I shuffled along behind Nikki. She opened the door and I let go of her hand to grab my father's bulky survival kit flashlight. I grasped it tightly as we slid out the front door, careful to close the door slowly so it didn't squeak or slam shut.

Outside the children were already waiting for us. Without a campfire to sit by, the summer night air chilled me through my pajamas. Nikki smiled at the other children, but I stared down at the cold damp grass. I didn't want to step on any prickly weeds or stones.

"We decided to play Hide and Seek," said one of the kids, a little girl about Nikki's age. Her wet, stringy hair was tied up in pigtails.

"That's my favorite!" squealed Nikki.

The two of us looked back to our parents' bedroom window. No lights switched on to end our game. Relieved, my sister began looking around for hiding places. Her blond hair swished back and forth. I shivered and wished I had slipped shoes on.

A tall boy, next to the girl with pigtails, pointed at me. "Adam's going to be It."

"We decided," said another child, whose T-shirt was dripping.

"Yeah, he's It," Pigtails said.

I clung to the flashlight with my clammy hands. I felt everyone's eyes on me.

"How many are playing?" I said, looking around at the children. They moved about, and, in the dark, I couldn't tell how many there were. We only came up to the cottage once a year, and I had never met anyone else up here.

Pigtails glared at me. "Everyone," she said. "Go and count." Her pale, pruny finger pointed to the end of the dock. It stuck out over the dark lake.

"How high should I count?"

"As high as you want. Just count," said my sister before she dashed across the grass with the others. Her lavender sleep shirt fluttered over her knees in the breeze.

I crept out onto the dock, which groaned under my

weight. The water gurgled against the dock's posts. I began counting quietly, but the numbers still echoed over the open water until the night swallowed them.

"Nine. Ten. Eleven."

I squeezed my eyes shut even when the creaking wooden dock swayed beneath my feet.

"Seventeen. Eighteen."

I hoped I could find Nikki and we could go back inside.

"Thirty. Thirty-one."

Something splashed in the open water next to me, splattering my toes with frigid lake water.

"Forty-five. Forty-six."

I'd lost track of the echoing giggles of the other children.

"Fifty." I still held tight to the flashlight. It was slippery in my hands. I peeked at the black water, worried I might drop the flashlight into it.

"Fifty-seven?" I looked around. Empty.

"Fifty-eight, fifty-nine, sixty. Um, ready or not," I said to the chill summer air. I clicked the flashlight on. The beam illuminated a face in the inky lake water. I stumbled backwards and the flashlight clunked onto the dock. I heard something large emerging from the water while I reached for the flashlight. I held it out in front of me like a sword.

"You found me." The tall boy from before spat out water so he could laugh at me. "You should have seen your face."

"Well, that's one," I muttered. *Where was Nikki?* The silence weighed down the night as I looked for the others. The tall boy followed me. His wet shoes squeaked in the grass. I grew more chilly as I searched. My only light swept back and forth. I felt like a policeman or maybe some kind of monster hunter as I squinted into the cattails along the side of the lake.

A pair of eyes stared back.

"You!" I squeaked as the girl with pigtails jumped out. Her bare feet splashed in the mud. She didn't say anything, but she did smile and silently follow me like the other boy.

After what felt like an hour, my toes were freezing. I'd found two other children. I think. I kept losing count. I still hadn't found my sister.

"Come on, Nikki. Where are you?"

"You'll never find her," said the children behind me.

I stopped and turned to look at them. Under my light, they still looked soaking wet.

"We told her the best place to hide," said one boy.

"We can give you a hint," said the girl with pigtails.

"Please?" I asked.

I just wanted to go inside. I didn't care if hints were cheating. The children walked closer to me. They all moved together. I stepped back, but they kept coming toward me. My foot touched the slippery mud on the edge of the lake. The tall boy stepped up and placed two hands on my shoulders. He shoved me back.

"Just go look."

I fell into the black lake. Despite the cold air, the water was warm and smooth. My arms and legs fumbled for the lake bottom, but all I found was seaweed. I was sinking. I heard the children's garbled voices.

"You're It."

"You have to go find her."

"She's all the way down."

Pyrite

Katy Hojnacki

We got left behind in a town named for fool's gold. The town stripped the mines bare over thirty years ago, and with their entrances collapsed, its deadbeat residents didn't use them for shelter against the harsh desert sun.

We know the town better because it sounds like pirate, which best describes the demeanor of the locals. Staying out of sight of the street, we follow patches of shade throughout the day. No one here would hesitate to mug a bunch of teenagers—we're an opportunity for supplies, however minimal ours are.

Exposed metal beams in the old industrial town turn the empty buildings into ovens. The sand and sun scour everything they touch. All day, we bake like bread in the heat. After dusk, we fight off the desert chill by taking advantage of the leftover warmth inside those buildings before the night steals it away. We make wimpy fires out of fast-burning, desiccated wood. The short-lived flame is a mixed blessing. No one wants a fire long enough for the locals to spot us.

Our canteens are empty.

The rainwater deposits I know of are dry. I wait until my cousin is asleep before I sneak off. I have to slip out before she stirs or I'll get an earful, and her hoarse yelling is only going to remind me how low our water supply is. There's one spot that may still be stocked—a cistern near the fig trees on the west edge of town.

Night gives me cover, preventing the locals from catching sight of my tell-tale red cowl. So long as I keep a look out for the wildlife, I can cross the town square unbothered in the dark and make my way to the fig trees, and, more importantly, the water storage in the rocks nearby.

I heave the stone covering the cistern. Deep down inside, the moonlight glints on the meager water supply. I tighten a fraying rope on my canteen and drop it down the hole. The container catches on the rope before hitting the bottom, so I can lower it down. I hear it scrape against the stone floor and hope it can partially fill. When I lift the rope again, the canteen is heavier than I expected, which is a relief.

As I untie the rope to attach it to fill another container, I shudder, noting a silhouette on the flat sands. The only man I can figure who would travel at night is the town Gatekeeper—the last person I would want to find me leeching the water supply.

I slide my feet into the cistern opening and drop in, my fingers clinging to the edges of the entry hole. My arms and legs instantly chill. My hands stiffen. I curse as I hear running footsteps heading in my direction; the sound echoes in the vacuous cistern I hang in. They slow upon reaching the hole, and a bright flashlight beam blinds me when I look up sheepishly.

"A damn burner? Really?" He snorts and kicks dust in my eyes. "Thought your gang of redcloaks all left after Aduro got ganked."

"Most of them did," I say. Feeling the sand scratching my eyes, I squint and glare back at him.

"And here I thought the neighborhood was cleaning up," responds the Gatekeeper. His sun-wrinkled face scowls down at me for a moment before cracking into a smirk. "Guess you don't get rations anymore, huh?"

I don't reply, more focused with keeping my fingers

gripping the dusty edge of the cistern. I should have just run.

"You're that Ígnea boy, ain't you? Diego, right? Your sister's a hell of a catch. I'm sure we could make a deal if water's all you're looking for."

"Cousin," I correct him. My stomach twists as the rough treads of the Gatekeeper's boots rest on my fingers.

"Gimme one reason not to break your fingers, shitstain."

I swallow, my throat dry as the sand the Gatekeeper stands on. My feet swing, groundless, as I try to remember how much rope it took to get my canteen to the bottom. I look down, but it's too dark to see the water's surface now that I block the moonlight.

"You don't want a corpse in your drinking water," I say quietly, but the empty cistern echoes my response. I feel my fingers slipping.

The Gatekeeper grunts, grabs me by the wrist, and heaves me out of the hole.

"Get your ass out of here, Diego," he says, "and make sure the lot of you die where I don't have to clean it up."

The Dance

Katy Hojnacki

"Look, I told you I was only with you until the Fringe,"
said Besmahs. The slim man moved past the crumbling, stone
border wall of the tiny town.

"I don't have my quarry, elf," growled Yngor, sliding off
his horse. His thick feet thudded on the ground, and his
armor clinked on impact. The barbarian jabbed his blotchy
nose close to the elf's smooth, angular face. "You stick with
me until his head is in my hands."

His skin looked as beaten as his armor, a savage collage of
hide, bone, and scraps of steel.

"You hired me to pursue," Besmahs said, "not to catch."
He turned his attention to a woman approaching from the
town. The harsh sun cast deep shadows on the meager, well-
weathered buildings behind her. She wore loose-fitting orange
robes and a warm smile.

"Refugees?" she asked pleasantly, either unaware or
choosing not to acknowledge the palpable fury in Yngor's
posture.

"I am," said Besmahs, approaching her.

"Should have known better than to hire a brittle-boned
tree folk!" said Yngor. "You vagabonds are a waste of coin."

"You are all welcome to join the festivities," said the
woman, frowning, "refugee or not." Her face brightened, her
deep brown skin shone in the sun. "Come, the dancing

begins soon."

Behind her, people in brightly colored clothing gathered at the base of a wide, short building. Their flowing capes and sweeping skirts caught the elf's eye.

"Come now, Yngor," said Besmahs with a dismissive wave of his hand. The delicate gesture brought a disgusted look to the barbarian's scarred face. Besmahs found it satisfying. "You and yours love merriment as much as anyone." With a smirk, he added, "Besides, ladies love a man who can dance."

The elf sauntered alongside the woman from town. She held out her hands, but when Besmahs reached to accept the invitation, she dropped a stone medallion into his palm.

"For refugees," whispered the woman as Besmahs put on the medallion. The smooth amulet felt cool and light, chilling his chest.

Yngor narrowed his eyes, but followed after he retrieved the horse. He walked it to the edge of the crowd. Sweat seeped into his beard as he scowled at the joyous gathering.

Several people holding flutes, drums, and bells made up the crowd. They gathered around a circular stage with a stone base. Wooden plank stairs spiraled up its edge. A pillar stood at the northern end, emblazoned with a gleaming, golden clock. The time was nearly noon. For a moment, the noise of conversation dwindled.

As the clock's hand ticked noon, the beating of drums erupted.

Music pulsed the group to life as they bounded up the stairs to the stage. A stranger in a golden dress linked arms with Besmahs and carried him with her. He had little objection to joining the throng as they leapt and twirled. He spun and changed partners, flashing smiles and stealing glances. The dancers spread apart and joined together as naturally as breathing. Flesh brushed up against flesh, and capes and dresses swished as they passed.

Vivid reds and olive greens popped from the swirling

skirts. Orange and gold fabrics swept like fires to the songs. The smell of sunshine and fresh air invigorated the dance, and the music carried on for hours.

Besmahs had curled his arm around the hips of several pretty prospects, but none would leave the stage. They shared a smoldering gaze, an ephemeral closeness, and a capricious farewell before disappearing into the dance.

His muscles ached, but the pounding of the drum demanded stomping feet. The beat bled into the boards, each bounce binding the dancers here. The lilting flutes twirled the ladies and mandolin melodies moved the men. The elf could not bring himself to stop.

With the sun setting, Besmahs was growing impatient. He had long lost sight of anything off the stage, Yngor included. The elf adjusted his step and slid his hand down a woman's back. When she spun, he was surprised to see a friend, not a conquest. Her slanted, green eyes and elongated ears sang the far cry of a lost home.

"Besmahs? Is that you?" she said as Besmahs pulled his hand back.

"Kaeriel! What are you doing here?" He said, tightening the circle of his dance to remain near her.

Her long fingers pulled at something on her neck, and she revealed a stone medallion. Smiling, Besmahs did the same. His gaze savored Kaeriel's familiar features. Her bronze skin and dark, silky hair brought him comfort after so many months of the local pink-skinned, straw-haired folk.

"Shall we share a proper dance, then?" said Kaeriel with a friendly jab to the elf's ribs.

"Yes, a proper dance," he agreed as the two joined.

Besmahs and Kaeriel shared a grace unlike the other dance partners on the stage. They danced a seemingly superfluous flurry of footwork, melding in a remembered melody. They improvised from the beats, recalling old Elven tunes close enough to tie to the music around them. Many eyes turned to the pair, including the now pacified gaze of the mighty Yngor.

The pair of elves promised to end their dance with the conclusion of the next song, but the melodies carrying the dance were an endless medley. No one had left the floor in hours. Sunset turned to darkness, and tired legs turned to aching feet. Their friendly touch had grown tighter with concern. The crowd remained cramped while the clock crept later.

As the clock's hand struck midnight, the music halted. Besmahs and Kaeriel stood alone in the chilled, night air. Their medallions fell and struck the wooden floor between them like two drum beats.

Kalle Kivi

Kalle Kivi is a poet and writer who enjoys traveling, gardening, and Michigan's four seasons. He's written for the Michigan Citizen, the Detroit River Current Newsletter, and was a part of the writing team for the Detroit River American Heritage Initiative.

He was a GED Instructor and worked in education community development for 25 years. As project manager working with teens and young adults, his group created community gardens and public murals in Southwest Detroit.

Kivi was Co-Chair of the Friends of the Detroit River and worked on parks and greenway development, pollution prevention and special events planning as an active community organizer and lobbyist. He is a graduate of the University of Michigan and Utica High School.

The Better Stuff
Kalle Kivi

Old Satan did arrange a date

Between ignorance and hate

They twisted while they trysted

Never thought to hesitate

A child to which they gave birth

Became known o'er all the Earth

Racism took its name

Pain and misery its big claim

Travelling throughout the land

Causing folks to take a stand

Against people they just don't know

Tricking others that this is so

One day good people called his bluff

For too long they had had enough

Delusion and confusion

Finding Love, the better stuff

Giving… Thanks

Kalle Kivi

Welcome to these eastern shores, Ghazwan of Iraq
to peninsulas by fresh waters, verdant trees, many colored delight
from deserts of your home, cradled valleys of yore
May you find respite from terror, of too many years at war
of twisted ideas, evil lies, seeds of crime

Welcome to these western shores, Le Van Toc of Vietnam
carrying memories of people too many years fought and died
for freedom to live, to grow happy dreams expressed
Into this melting pot of generations, a mixed salad bowl dressed
with ingredients that nourish our many one souls

Welcome to these sanctuary shores, Albert of Germany
escaping tattoos of hatred, declared by hunger, bullets, ovens
liberate and flourish your growing genius within
A will to see beyond despair, destruction of the immediate, of sin
free to create proofs of the universal sublime

Beware the welcome to these foreign shores, Nkenge of Africa
respecting dear ancestors once forced from village to come
against their spirited will in darkness of night
Yet still summon profound dignity, courage to resist, to fight
contradicted ideas of equality--happiness pursued goals

Original people of Iroquois Nation, the Aztec, Lakota, and Carib
long ago welcomed strangers who settled your home shores
for which they gave you and their gods many thanks
While bringing diseases, manifest destiny, deceit in the rank.
May your survival be a testament for all time

Flyby

Kalle Kivi

Two neighbors walked slowly, side by side, into an open field
under sunset sky, a crisp December joy

Taking a break from yard clean-up chores, enjoying being
out-of-doors, to view a special heavenly event

The International Space Station, he told her proudly, is
supposed to be visible tonight, in ten minutes at 5:25

Where do we look, she asked, bored; How well will we see it?
And look at that beautiful sunset!

Over there, from west southwest to east northeast, he
pointed up. Weatherman said for four minutes

A twinkling light appeared certain, from that very direction,
well above a horizon with no stars yet aglow

Is it the Space Station or an airplane? They asked each other;
Metro Airport is sorta kinda in that direction

After the first minute both knew; this object moved with different bearing, relatively higher through the sky

Blink, blinking brighter--tearing faster as it approached overhead; a steady pace of no distinct shape or size

Backlit by the setting sun, soaring higher than any simple jet; leaving a faint streak not a thicker jet entrail

The two acquaintances shared their second minute in silent awe, experiencing the remote mystery fly by

With a speed of five miles per second, according to the weatherman, he did some mental math to tell her

This definitely I.S.S. will travel 1200 miles in our four minutes of sight, at speed of 18,000 miles per hour flight

Who is on board; how'd they get to ride, she asked? Five astronauts, he said: 2 American, 2 Russian, 1 Italian

I hope they don't fuss and fight, she replied, work together, settle differences without violence or prejudice

Two friends walked slowly home, hand in hand; the twinkling craft receded, on time along its destined path

Faint light was all he needed when he looked so closely, to see her happy eyes sparkle back a pleasant thought

Over a subtle grin, come on inside, she said, we can relax over hot chocolate because I've got some questions

Is there a lady or two among the five astronauts? Has anyone, you know, ever "done the deed" in space?

Looking away from her dancing eyes, I don't know, he grinned: anything in the good name of science!

Zero gravity would be a hoot, two explorers giggled and agreed, would be a tight fit—but ooh the possibilities

I'm not sure, but I think both a man and a woman have spent a whole year in space, but not at the same time

Good thing, she reasoned, if they weren't compatible he couldn't just run off and she couldn't throw him out

Inching closer with shared resolve, he opened, "I won't run off"… "I won't throw you out!" she assured

A slight nod toward the hallway, she led him "Tis the season—love thy neighbor"; "For Science," his reply

Two lovers roused slowly awake, secure in their shelter from early winter wind on this now starry night

Tell me about those books you read, she asked, one called *The 7 Daughters of Eve*, the other *Almost Human*.

Some 2000 generations spanning 25 years per have passed since we modern humans thought consciously

How we clanned together in caves, learning to use that special sharp stone to scrape meat from the bone

Struggling to understand why and then to ritually bury together our loved ones of all ages once dead

Tonight we saw people flying high in a tin can, while mere humans still strain to live in peace here on earth

Trying to best use our vast technological advances as we lag far behind in spiritual and social development

However, sweet lady, we sure made it, together tonight, pondering what is best within this universe of stars

She turned ever so slowly, pressing her naked warmth against him once more, offering a soft kiss to his chest

Their understanding eyes met in eternal distant closeness, her sweet whisper trailing away, "Why thank you…"

Rebecca Eve Schweitzer

Rebecca Eve Schweitzer is a writer, editor, blogger, social media manager, marketing consultant and word nerd based in the Metro-Detroit area. She is a member of the Tuesday Morning Writers and the Sterling Heights Creative Writers Workshop. Her blog about culture, women's history and writing can be found at beccaeve.com.

The Bird Days of Summer

Rebecca Eve Schweitzer

Maybe I've watched too many Hitchcock movies. Perhaps I've spent too much time in the heat. It's probably just my imagination. The odd cawing. The spooky swooping. The eerie death toll. Three dead birds in my path, mangled by Michigan summer, within less than half a mile of each other. The first bird had little left. The bones and meat were gone, leaving mostly feathers splayed out and still shaped like a bird in its own crime scene chalk line. The second bird was scattered—a wing here, a foot there. The third bird, a pile of feathers like the first. I wondered if they were all the same bird. A second lap of the route uncovered four beaks. Either a carnival sideshow died undiscovered, or four dead birds crowded my loop around the neighborhood.

This could all be the fault of a full moon. Maybe someone is putting poison in a bird bath.

I might have moved on and forgotten about my morning counting bird beaks. I might have been able to blame Ms. McGinty's ratty cat. That is, until the birds started falling out of the sky.

* * *

Nobody shot it. The sparrow was flitting from tree to tree, chirping. It stretched out to span the length of the street toward a stately old oak when it just fell. It wasn't a nose dive. No shot took it off its course. It belly flopped right to the pavement. It pancaked. Its little skull caved in. Anyone finding it on the street would have thought it laid down, wings out, and waited for a car to drive over it. Only its beak remained intact.

Five.

It remained untouched for three days until the rain washed it aside. Even McGinty's old ratty catty turned down the free meal. Too flattened, maybe. Or the cat knew something we didn't. I called the city when the death toll reached seven. All seven beaks were still discoverable. They didn't seem interested. They asked what I had been feeding the birds. I mentioned avian flu. They told me not to touch the carcasses. I mentioned a news reporter. They sent someone out to clean up and test the birds.

The next morning three birds, sparrows, waited on my car. One on the hood ornament. The other two on either side view mirror. The middle bird made a guttural noise.

Certain I'd lost my mind, I responded, "Tell me what thy lordly name is on the Night's Plutonian shore." I half expected it to answer, "Nevermore." Instead, it nodded at me then at the other two birds. They flew off in unison.

I couldn't tell if the birds meant to give a threat or an olive branch. But either would have been delivered by vultures or doves respectively. What did sparrows mean? I wondered if I should consult an ornithologist. Then I wondered if I should consult a psychologist. The latter seemed a wise choice, but owls would have meant wisdom so I drove to the library instead.

The library revealed the sparrow as a symbol of hope and renewal. The dead robin I found was a similar symbol of hope, renewal, and coming warmth. None of this made any sense, not that it should. I carried my bird books to the checkout counter. As I waited in line, I envisioned my future—the bird conspiracy theorist. Years from now, after swerving to miss a bird in the road, I'd be dead, and they'd come clean out my house. My sister would complain about the mess and my packrat tendencies. My nephew would revel in the inherited hobby tools. My niece would fight with him over the vast collection of electronics. And the whole bunch would stand in terror when they opened the door to my study finding dead bird photos, news clippings, souvenir feathers—all documented, pinned up, and linked together with color-coded string—the collection of a madwoman, a Chicken Little who thought the sky was falling.

I left the library without the books, plopped right on the floor in the spot I'd been standing as though I meant for them to save my place in line. I walked out the door, down the front steps and right on to the freshly oozing, spread-eagled, pancake-flat carcass of a blue jay.

* * *

Some city health official named Martina called to tell me the birds came back clean—no avian flu. I asked about poison. She said nothing unusual showed up, which means they didn't check. She said it was probably neighborhood cats. Maybe kids. She said it could even be the heat. She then asked how much time I'd been spending out in the heat. I asked if there had been any signs of *foul* play. She hung up.

* * *

The next day, the carcasses were gone. I spent the morning scanning the ground. By afternoon, I wondered if I would be recognized at the library if I went back for the books. It wasn't until evening, when I looked up at the purple red sunset that I noticed it—no birds on the wires, no birds backlit by the setting sun, no birds chirping over the sea. I wondered, hoped they all went to bed early.

I woke up missing something the next morning, but not sure what. The world felt less heavy but also less bright. The morning sun rose to light my front windows. I poured my coffee and walked outside to fetch my newspaper. I stood in the morning air, listening to wind chimes jingle in the breeze. My neighbor walked out for his paper as the air stilled. I noticed it then, the quiet.

My neighbor waved, and I walked toward him.

"Do you hear that?"

"Hear what?" he said.

"The quiet."

"Ah," he breathed out, satisfied. "I love the quiet of the mornings."

"The birds are gone."

"Birds? What are birds?"

Matryoshka

Rebecca Eve Schweitzer

When they finally split you open, they will find a smaller you—perfectly proportioned, just smaller. Doctors will demand tests. News crews will hound you. And religious groups will denounce you. Until they all forget about you and move on.

The slightly smaller version of you will crack one day, and one smaller still will emerge. They'll compare tests. The story will baffle. Networks will offer you a reality show. You'll accept because it's getting difficult to reach the top shelf.

The third break will happen on camera. Once again, the tests will show a normal, just smaller, human—nothing special, which is accurate. The news will recycle their headlines. Conspiracy theories will take center stage, and a cult will worship you. The network will renew your show at a million per episode. Smaller you will buy a bigger house.

When it turns out you can't shed your skin on demand, the network will cancel. The cameras will stop. The medical profession will doubt any of it happened. And the circus sideshows will have a newer, weirder novelty. You won't even be asked to host a game show. The unofficial cult of you will limp along until people slice themselves open, expecting to find a smaller version inside.

You'll convince a doctor to try exploratory surgery despite the ethics. It will work. A fourth version—still you, still not special—will start it all over again. This time, though, they will want answers.

Versions five through nine will arrive in rapid succession. Without your consent, you're too small to be human anymore—empty you after empty you will line up in a laboratory. Advocates will try to free you, and the religious groups will try to outlaw you. Politicians won't comment on you.

They will keep unwrapping you, lining up your remains, looking for tinier instruments. You'll protest, but you'll be too small. And there will be too many of you for them to stop now.

So, it will continue.
Until you stop showing up in pictures.
Until you might no longer really be there.
Until someone thinks to ask, years after the fact,
where are you now?

John Castellenas

Born in Detroit, John Castellenas has been writing for almost 50 years. He believes writing and reading is needed to make us understand our world.

Castellenas lives in Clinton Township, Michigan.

A Spring Flower

John Castellenas

Was a Spring flower,
so bright and so beautiful,
reaching for the sky and
the sky and the sun adored her.

She would dance with the wind and
the wind would whisper love songs to her.
Late Summer came and the flower slowly weakened
and faded away.
The sky cried great rain/snow and the sun hid
behind the clouds.
In early Spring,
the flower appeared.

The rain and snow stopped and
the sun shined from morning dawn to nightly dusk.
The gentle wind danced with the beautiful flower and
the world became beautiful and wonderful once again.

The Lover (A Soldier Prayer)

John Castellenas

Poor boys and men.
Their roads lead to War.

Young woman with a sweet smile.
Silk dress.
Smelling like Spring flowers.

She whispered, "Let us dance tonight.
You shall go to War and tonight we need to create
photos for the heart. Memories to keep you warm
when you are lonely and afraid."

Young man brought the woman close.
Whispered kind words of love and thankfulness.

A soldier stands alone and
he is cleaning his M-16.
Death is all around him.

He closes his eyes.
He remembers.
The smell of flowers.
The feel of the silk dress.

The sweet smile of his love.

Keeps him human.

Wild Roses

John Castellenas

I know the wild rose.
Her beauty had tempted me for many months and
she would dance with me when the songs were good.
She was a long legged woman who had wild blue eyes and
loved the whiskey and the long night.

I loved her auburn hair and her kind and sweet voice.
 She often told me.
 "Wild roses grow where they want. They know pretty lies
and stories The wild rose grows near the river and the thorns
can make you bleed for the remnant of love that is left. It lulls
the breath of wishes, that cannot be fulfilled. Old lovers may
weep but the wild rose cannot."

I told her often. Free men fear not the wild roses. The taste
of the sweet kiss and the loving embrace would be enough.
Heavy darkness and desperate loneliness become the night
when a lover's wish is not fulfilled. Love is sweet and can be
very dangerous. You will bleed and weep for love often.
Better to have slow danced and known the gentle touch of
the wild rose. Men, who do not know the blushing rose, they
yearn for the dance with the wild rose always.

She smiled and whispered. "Brave soldier who fear not the
night nor the ending. You shall know the deep sadness one
day. The wild roses are free and men want to hold and
control all things. I shall break your heart."

I brought her closer, I knew her words were true and I still
loved and needed my wild rose.

Tony Aued

Tony Aued is a retired local teacher living in Macomb County. He loved teaching and still enjoys mentoring young writers with school visits. He and his wife, Kathy, have been married 48 years and have two children. One is a newspaper editor in Georgia and the other is a yoga and trapeze performer in California.

His first published novel, *Blair Adams, The Package*, was released in 2005, since then he has written seven novels. The first four FBI Thrillers, are about a female agent thrust into cases which cross the country. In 2012, he introduced us to Detroit Detective Don Frederickson, who is the main character in the Motor City Murder Series. The four books, anchored by *Murder in Greektown*, have been awarded, Amazon Best Sellers. He just finished the fourth book in the local series, *Revenge in the Motor City*. It takes the reader on a ride through both Wayne and Macomb Counties with scenes taking place in St. Clair Shores and the Eastern Market.

Tony will be appearing at over twenty local events; as well as, book signings across the country. His novels are available on Tonyaued.com , Amazon Books, and many local bookstores.

The Collector

Tony Aued

Mark Baxter and his wife Cindy had been married nineteen years, and he knew she was the perfect person for him. The couple settled in a quaint subdivision, Shady Lane Village. It would be a great neighborhood for them. Rolling hills and tree lined streets with children playing ball in the park that bordered the ranch style homes were the best place to bring up a family. Although the two Baxter children were now in high school, Mark had loving memories of tossing a baseball with their two boys after coming home from a hard day at the office. Now those memories were washed away in tears of doubt. Just how long had his wife been cheating on him?

Mark wanted to make sure his suspicions were right. He slumped in the front seat of the rental vehicle he picked up, planning to spy on his wife. Both of their boys were off at camp for the week, and Cindy would be home alone. It was four in the afternoon, and he'd normally be at work, not expected to be home for at least two more hours. There had been late night phone calls. They always hung up when he answered. What else could have been going on? He questioned his wife, but she didn't seem concerned. The last question in his mind was who? Who was his wife cheating with?

That's when he saw the man coming out of the garage. He

sat up. *Shit!* Mark couldn't believe it was his next door neighbor, and now he's coming out the side door of Mark's home. John Daily, a good looking younger guy, someone that Mark considered a friend, now walked out of Mark's side door, looking back and forth, appearing secretive, like he didn't want anyone to spot him. Mark watched as John moved down the street to his own garage. It took everything he could muster not to jump out of his vehicle and punch the daylights out of the man. Why would Cindy do this? He was sure that it wasn't anything he did, but it was his wife that was to blame.

In the past, John and Mark would sit in that same garage looking at their collection of baseball cards. Both men were proud of the pristine older cards that pictured sports heroes of times past. It would seem like a competition at times, especially when John saw that Mark had both Mickey Mantle and Henry Aaron rookie cards. Mark smiled when John nearly fell off his seat when he saw the two special baseball cards. Even though they were valuable, the main point was how rare they were. Now Mark watched John and wondered how long this had gone on with his wife. It was a couple months ago when Mark first suspected his wife seeing another man. One time he came home early and she was out. When he asked, her excuses were flimsy. She'd say, "just went for a walk." She never liked walking, but maybe she was hoping to get a little exercise. Whatever her reason, he'd let it go, but now it all fit together. A few weeks ago he saw her outside talking to John. The two of them acted oddly when he walked over to join them. He was putting it together. They were up to something. Mark planned to stop it.

The Dailys and Baxters were friends, that is until John and his wife divorced. When John and his wife had troubles, the Baxters tried not to take sides. John's wife soon moved out and the Baxters felt sorry for John. They'd try to keep a relationship but it became harder with John's wife gone. Mark wondered why John's marriage broke up. Could it be that John and Cindy had been having an affair for a while? Did John's wife find out? Mark knew that she moved back to Chicago where she was originally from. If he knew where, he'd call her to see what she knew. Mark was certain that John was the one coming between him and his wife.

It was after six, the normal time that Mark would be expected to come home from work. Mark had plans, but he wasn't ready to put them in gear. Pulling in his driveway, he grabbed his briefcase and entered the kitchen. Cindy was standing at the sink, washing veggies for a salad. He watched her turn and smile, and she leaned over to give her husband a kiss. Even as she planted one on his cheek, he stepped back and looked at her. Thinking, how could she cheat on him?

Clearing his throat, he asked, "What's for dinner?"

She told him she had spaghetti on the stove. Nodding, he walked into the living room. Mark was in the bedroom when he heard her tell him that dinner would be ready in a few minutes.

"I'll be there in a minute." It was time for Mark to put his plans into action. He came into the kitchen, "Hey, I saw John outside when I pulled in. How about I call and ask him to join us? Hope that's okay."

Cindy was surprised, but agreed that it would be nice. Mark continued talking, "Yeah, I thought we needed to make sure he was okay, and I hadn't seen him for a while. How about you?" She didn't answer, but moved back to the stove. He said, "Glad you made something that would be enough for three of us." John was disappointed that she didn't have more of a reaction and added, "We hadn't seen him in a while." He waited for her response. "Cindy, sure haven't you talked to him?"

Cindy turned to the cupboard, "No, it's been weeks since I've seen him." She started to get out another place setting for the additional guest. The lack of any other reaction from her disappointed him. He watched his wife re-set the table for the additional dinner guest.

He continued asking her leading questions. "Maybe John isn't going to want to stay in the neighborhood. Bet he'll put their place up for sale."

She looked back at him. "Yeah, that kinda makes sense. Glad you invited him over." Hearing the doorbell, she headed to let their guest in.

Mark watched her heading to the door, hoping to catch both of them trying to get out of his web. He followed her to the door.

"Hey John, glad you could join us. How are you doing, old pal?" Patting his neighbor on the back, he said, "Come on, sit down. Cindy makes great spaghetti. Maybe you've had it before?"

John looked back to Cindy first, then answered, "No, don't think so, but I appreciate the invitation. Always glad to have a home cooked meal." With a puzzled expression, he peeked back at Cindy again.

She shook her head, shrugging her shoulders.

John took a deep breath, not sure what was going on, he asked, "So, Mark, what have you been up to?"

They were all now seated at the table and Mark just stared at his neighbor for a few seconds before answering.

"Been pretty busy at work, wish I could get home earlier every night." He watched for any sign from either Cindy or John, but neither of them seemed to notice. Cindy passed the salad bowl to her husband, and he took it, thinking about the two of them being together. Now he would expose their affair. Mark cleared his throat, deciding to come out with it. He raised his voice and he pursed his lips before pounding on the table. The plates and silverware rattled, "I know about the two of you!" Mark stood, reaching into his pocket, and exposing a gun. "I'm on to you! I've known about your affair!" Mark was standing and slammed his chair into the table. John leaned back, falling out of his seat, crawling away from the screaming man who was waving the gun.

John yelled, "What the hell are you talking about? There's no affair going on." He was trying to crawl away but Mark stopped him.

"Stay right there!" He turned his attention to his wife. "Get up, move over next to your boyfriend."

Both of them did as requested. She tried to reason with her husband, "Honey, nothing's going on. We're not having an affair. Why would you think that?"

"I've seen you and John together, and today he was sneaking out of our house when I'm supposed to be at work. I've suspected something for over a month. There's all those late night calls." He was waving the gun, first pointing it at his neighbor then at Cindy. "I'm not an idiot. I saw both of you again this afternoon. I know you're having an affair."

Cindy looked at John, who was still on the floor, crawling backwards. She shouted, "Mark, I can explain." Before she could say another word, the blast from the gun stunned her, creating a loud ringing noise that pierced the quiet evening. Grabbing her ears, she turned, seeing blood pour out of John's chest. A second blast followed, striking the man on the ground, this time in the face. Blood pooled on the light tan carpeting, and Cindy screamed, crawling on the floor.

"Mark, what have you done?" She looked over, realizing that John was dead and figured she'd be next. Holding her hands up in front of her face, "Mark, you killed him. I'm not having an affair."

He was still pointing the gun at her. "You think I'm an idiot, I've seen you two together when I'm not home."

She was shaking, holding her hands up. "Sure, he's been here, but John's been helping me. I just wanted to surprise you for our anniversary."

Mark was still pointing the gun at his wife, and stuttered, "Helping you surprise me?"

Cindy had tears running down her face and was crying uncontrollably on the floor. "What do you mean, surprise me?" He moved closer to his wife, holding the weapon but now to his side, not sure what she was trying to tell him. He yelled, "Cindy, what in the hell is going on?"

"Mark," she could hardly speak, taking deep breaths, "John was helping me find the one baseball card that you've always talked about."

"Baseball card?"

"Yes, I asked him to help me find the Al Kaline rookie card that you've always wanted."

He was stunned, not sure what to do, "Kaline," he muttered. Looking down, he saw his wife crawling toward John, blood pouring out of his body.

"You killed him!"

The sound of sirens filled the otherwise quiet neighborhood outside. The loud sounds of gunfire brought panic to the normally sleepy street. Police officers now were outside, the demands were clear.

"Police, come out with your hands up!"

Mark dropped the gun, falling to his knees, "What have I done?"

The voices outside were louder, "You need to come out now, or we're coming in."

Mark was on his knees as Cindy moved to the door, opening it. Officers rushed in, taking hold of the man on his knees stooped down on the floor. Cindy explained what had happened to one of them as Mark was handcuffed and placed in the backseat of a squad car. As one of the officers covered the body of John Daily, neighbors gathered outside, one of them could be heard saying, "I thought they were a happy couple."

Another neighbor was heard saying, "Guess you never know what's going on next door."

Weam Namou

Weam Namou is an Eric Hoffer award-winning author of 12 books, a speaker, journalist, and filmmaker. She is vice president of Detroit Working Writers (DWW), a 118-year-old professional writing association, and an Ambassador for the Authors Guild of America, the nation's oldest and largest professional organization for writers.

A Mirror

Weam Namou

Seven gates lead into the Old City of Jerusalem, which is divided into Jewish, Muslim, Christian, and Armenian Quarters. Malika entered through the busiest one, Jaffa Gate, and a man approached her on David Street.

"You like me show you?" he asked in English, zigzagging his arm like a snake.

She didn't respond, but looked at him gently. He was in his thirties and as raggedy as an old carpet. Malika imagined a wife, five children, in-laws, one room.

The man took her silence to mean yes and led her to the Church of the Holy Sepulcher, built on the hill of Golgotha by Emperor Constantine in 335 over what was claimed to be the site of Jesus' crucifixion, burial, and resurrection. The bronze entrance door is surrounded with marble columns, and next to it is a sealed door. A Muslim family holds the key to the entrance and locks it every night, because the Christian sects cannot trust one another to hold it.

Once there, he asked if she wanted him to show her inside. She shook her head and he put his hand out. All she had in her purse was a hundred shekel coin.

"I give you change, I give you change," he said hurriedly, seeing her confused expression.

She gave him the money and he fled. Her lips quivering, she hated that this had happened here. Here is the church.

Muslim's third holiest shrine, The Dome of the Rock, shines here with its golden dome and tiled walls of many colors. And Judaism's most revered site, the last remaining portions of the ancient Temple of Solomon, called the Western or "Wailing" Wall, sits here.

Malika thought the man must have mistaken her for a rich tourist, not the native Palestinian she was. Without distinct physical traits or certain dress codes like military uniforms, veils or yamikas, identities weren't easily spotted in Jerusalem, even for the people born there. The capital of Israel, the ancient city of Palestine, was too diverse, packed with Christians, Jews, Muslims, and in the mid-afternoons, tourists.

Malika excused the man's behavior because she was good hearted. It wasn't his fault she didn't have typical Middle Eastern features. Instead, she had shoulder length reddish hair, was 5'4", medium-boned, fair skinned with freckles. She had plenty of curves, but the length and layers of her clothes hid them well, like pistachios in baklava.

"What, these people think they're entering a public bathhouse?" the Arabic guard at the entrance courtyard mumbled about the crowd of tourists walking into the church, dressed in tank tops and shorts.

Malika continued inside the church. She knelt in front of the Stone of Unction, where Jesus' body was anointed and wrapped after his death. She pressed her forehead against the wet stone. Immediately, there was peace. Malika asked for forgiveness, in case she'd hurt anyone in the past week, and in case she'd end up hurting anyone in the upcoming week. Then she lit candles.

Holding her green rosary, she said a Hail Mary and an Our Father. She apologized for not being able to donate today, given she was just robbed. She said a prayer for the world, the Middle East, Palestinians, her town Taybeh, family, friends, relatives, and one for the thief.

"May he enjoy every agorot of the hundred shekel," she said.

She touched the unopened envelope that she'd placed in her skirt's pocket. It arrived this morning but she waited to read it. She already had an idea what the sender, Nadir, wrote. Without revealing his gender, he would give his regards, and persuade her to soon visit his father's jewelry store where he worked.

"Dear Jesus, guide me to what to do about Nadir," Malika whispered.

Malika met Nadir two years ago, and from the start knew he was Muslim. Aware of the consequences involved in courting a man of a different religion, she still fell in love with him.

Malika went inside the shrine of Jesus' Tomb after having stood in a long line of people. The moment she saw the candles, paintings of Jesus, the satin scarf and a vase of fresh lilies, her eyes teared. She stared at the marble slab—purposely cracked to deter Ottoman looters—that covered the rock on which Jesus' body was believed to have been laid.

Kissing the cold slab, she begged to be shown what to do in regards to Nadir, how to maintain him without losing her family or herself. Tears fell on the marble, her cheeks and fingers but she couldn't stir to wipe them. Minutes—she could not tell how many—passed before her thoughts dropped and a quietness presided. Then He spoke.

She was told not to worry, to surrender to the problem. When the wind blew, trees surrendered by waving. So did oceans and grass blades. If they didn't, they'd break. Malika finally got up and swept out of the church in a state of bliss. Everything around her floated like a ship. She knew she was gone, far far away, as she left the Old City through Bab Al-Amud.

She stopped at a coffee shop and asked the merchant to use the phone, to call her father to pick her up since she didn't have bus or taxi fare. The merchant invited her to a cup of chai and she gladly accepted. A nice old man, he reminded her of her childhood, their gardener Jabir with his yellow eyes and olive skin, his wrinkles and hollow mouth, his dark gallabeya, a long-sleeved, ankle-length shirt, and his white turban.

She remembered Uncle Jabir's Quranic verses, his prayer rug, his knowledge of earth. He attended to the apricot and lemon trees like they were his family. He taught her when and how to water plants and flowers and said quite a bit about her religion. She stood barefoot beside him, listening. By the time she'd re-entered her home, she had learned more about his Mohammad and her Jesus.

The idea of marriage was becoming more complicated every day, she thought, with gods, prophets, and parents involved. Perhaps she should become a nun, or abandon him. Perhaps she should spend more time understanding herself.

The Wordsmith's Purse

Weam Namou

Words, poems and stories
are packed in a purse that's in my head.
A purse that keeps getting crowded
with napkins, scrap paper, ticket stubs.
A purse bursting with words.

Poems and stories trickle here and there.
I attempt to pick up these words
and stuff them back into the purse.
Worry that some will be lost forever.
But my purse is bulging in pain
unable to keep the zipper zipped.
The snap closed, the fabric of the purse intact,
they want out. To pour over the world
and touch people's hearts.

They beg to be released and I take a pen
and paper and, one by one,
release them through lead and ink.

Talk to My Ancestor

Weam Namou

The minister called Jill, a churchgoer. A woman answered.

"Hi Jill, this is Reverend Elaine returning your call. About the —"

"Now let me stop you there," said the woman. "This is not Jill. It's her ancestor. Jill had to go take care of some business."

"Ok then I'll try calling her later." Reverend Elaine hung up.

The next day, Jill approached Reverend Elaine at church and said, "I thought this was a spiritualist church."

"It is."

"Then when you called yesterday, why did you not leave a message with my ancestor?"

"I called to speak to you, not your ancestor or anyone else."

This reminded Reverend Elaine of another story. One woman, whenever she asked her husband to do something, like take out the trash, she'd later learn that he didn't do it. Whenever she confronted him, he replied, "It wasn't me you were talking to. I was off on an emergency in the universe and one of my ancestors took my place."

Mary Rose Kreger

Mary is a young adult writer, wife, and new mom residing in Warren, Michigan. A lover of swords, Scotland, and adventures, Mary writes stories while her little one is napping. She is seeking publication for *Daughter of Avalon*, a YA fantasy revised with the help of one amazing editor and the Sterling Heights Creative Writers Workshop.

Mary's other writing projects include a sequel to *Daughter of Avalon*, as well as a memoir about the 19 months she spent in a convent before realizing she was called to marriage and family life—and to continue her writing journey.

Daughter of Avalon is currently available on SwoonReads.com.

Stories of Innocence and Experience

Mary Rose Kreger

The chalk-colored gravel and scrubby green cedar trees streaked by as Charles drove us down to Austin in his weathered tan Buick. Was this a date, or just a nice trip between two friends? I wasn't sure, but it felt like a date.

Just like the kiss Charles had given me last week (my first) had felt like a real kiss. Like maybe—no, almost certainly— Charles wanted to be more than friends.

Didn't a kiss mean something?

It's a date, I decided, fiddling with the pearl dangling from my gold-chained necklace. I glanced at Charles and perked up in my seat. *Of course it is. Right?*

The sweltering June heat greeted us as we hunted for a parking spot downtown. In Texas, the summer heat lingers deep into the night.

Charles took me to the Iron Cactus, where we ate chips and queso on the roof. The evening breeze kissed our cheeks, warm and moist as dragon's breath.

"Ugh, this heat!" I complained, drawing my sweat-frizzed hair into a tight bun. "It makes you miss those cool summer nights in Michigan, right?"

"Mmm," he agreed. We were both Michiganders, stranded in steamy central Texas.

I pulled my hand-me-down camera out of my purse. "May I?"

Charles nodded and shifted in the steel chair across from me, posing for my picture. His red T-shirt sported a black skull print encircled by rose petals. Death wreathed in beauty. It was a cool shirt, and a little strange. Unsettling.

I frowned as I gazed through the camera's viewfinder.

He's an atheist, Mary.

He gave me a sweet, boyish smile that didn't quite reach his pale blue eyes.

I clutched my camera tighter and swallowed.

I don't belong here. Not in Texas. And especially not with Charles.

My fingers squeezed the flash button, preserving the moment.

Whrr-click!

"So." He stretched leisurely in his seat. "What would you like to do next?"

"Well, this is Austin, isn't it?" I hid my camera away and leaned towards him with an eager grin. "The live music capital of the world? Let's go hear some tunes!"

We paid our bill and descended the stairs to Austin's "Dirty" Sixth Street. We ambled past a cluster of bars and restaurants, each bedecked with colorful strings of lights and flashing neon signs. The main drag was packed with motorcycles and rumbled with the sound of engines and bass guitars. Charles pulled me down a side alley, away from the crowded street. Dark ivy clung to the red brick building on our right as we passed through to the other side.

The room we entered was literally a big, ugly, hole-in-the-wall. There were no furniture or furnishings to speak of, just guests gathered around a heavy metal band jamming on the other side of the brick-and-concrete space.

The musicians hollered, screamed, and bounded across the stage with electrifying intensity. Their music roared wilder than their punk hairstyles and black leather getups. It reverberated deep in my chest, rattling my rib cage, like a fresh heartbeat invading me, body and soul. Each of my thrumming bones became their instruments.

Thud, thud, crash. Thud, thud, beat.

I forgot about the ugliness of my surroundings, and drank in that sound like it was my very own Elixir of Life. My ear drums rang, but I didn't care. As long as that beat pounded in my chest, I was feeling something inside. And as long as that beat went on, it was okay to feel. It was okay to feel angry.

Thud, thud, crash.

Hurt.

Thud, thud, beat.

Betrayed.

Thud, thud, crash-beat!

Alone.

Jim turning me away for Rosa. All the strained smiles and awkward meetings, the happy-for-them expressions that shocked and stung and tortured my weary spirit.

Angry. Hurt. Betrayed. Alone.

Thud, thud, crash-beat!

Charles' gaze flicked between me and the band. I smiled to let him know I liked it. I could not, and would not, tell him why.

When the music stopped, he took me up to meet the musicians. We met a taller, good-natured gentleman, and a sweet-but-fierce young lady. Both loud, unapologetic, melodic warriors.

"Here, let me take your picture." After a quick smile and a blinding camera flash, we said goodbye to the musicians and headed out on our own.

I didn't tell Charles about the storm brewing inside. I figured maybe he knew. I thought maybe that's why he was so kind, so gentle. He must have known about my broken heart.

Later, I followed his tall, loping figure down the city streets to his Buick.

Maybe Charles doesn't mind so much that I'm broken. I pictured

Jim Roberts in my mind: classy, handsome, a man of integrity.

I think Jim likes classy girls, my friend had warned. I patted down my frizzy hair and studied my unpainted fingernails.

Hmm. Not so classy. I chewed my lip, gazed again at Charles' steady figure. *But Charles doesn't mind.*

At that moment, he turned back towards me and grinned.

Heat rushed to my cheeks, and I fidgeted with the collar of my floral top.

The man was something of a mystery. What did I really know about Charles, except what he wanted me to see? The one thing I *did* know was that he believed almost the opposite of what I did. He thought God was a myth, and "if it feels good, it *is* good."

Yeah, but at least he's kind to me. I don't have to pretend around him.

I thought of his two tattoos—the peaceful snow leopard, and the demonic, snake-tongued skull. If I started dating Charles, which side of him would reign over our relationship?

The Texas swelter rustled the fringes of my top, pushing me towards Charles and the gloomy expanse of the city parking lot. Charles thumped the hood of his old Buick and watched my journey across the shadowed sidewalk.

"Ready for another long ride home?" His eyes sparkled, reflecting the amber glow of a distant streetlight.

"Ready," I agreed. As we drove home, I allowed myself to hope.

Maybe this was a date. Perhaps Charles and I could make things work. Maybe the snow leopard side would win.

Maybe... love would change everything.

Come and Find Me

Mary Rose Kreger

That night, Will Owain dreamed of a smoky room. Two sources of light in a damp, gloomy chamber: the first, a smoldering orange glow from a stone fireplace; the second, a pure white flame from an ivory candle.

Beside the candle, a fair hand composed a letter. Will could hear the scritch-scratch of the quill pen on the parchment.

Drip-drip. Water dripped somewhere in the gloom. A constant, irritating, *drip-drip-drip.*

The writer bent close to the candlelight. Will caught a glimpse of a pale, feminine face, shrouded by a tousled curtain of flame-red hair.

"Sweetheart," a voice mocked.

The writer hissed a curse and grabbed for the letter. In her haste, the quill and ink bottle crashed to the ground. Shards of glass and black ink splattered across the grimy stone floor.

In the dream, Will heard the jangle of keys and the shriek of metal grinding against metal.

The woman snatched up the letter and flung it into the fire.

Just as the door grated open, the woman placed herself before the fireplace. The firelight outlined her figure with an orange halo. Her faded dress was torn at the sleeves, revealing bruises and half-healed cuts up and down her emaciated arms. The woman's face was smudged with soot, but her eyes sparked like they, too, were heated by red-hot coals.

The woman was Will's *mother*.

A tall man with wispy white-blonde hair and eerie blue eyes marched into the room.

"My dearest Fiona." He smirked, revealing wolf-like teeth framed between waxy lips.

"Get out, Amaranth." Fiona ordered. Her slender figure shook with each word.

Amaranth glanced down at the shards of glass and the pool of ink on the floor. He rolled his eyes back towards Fiona.

"Where's the letter, sweetheart?" He fingered a knife on his belt and approached her.

Fiona held her position before the fireplace.

"No letter." She stretched out her hands. "Amaranth, please—"

Amaranth's backhand clipped the side of her head. He kicked her aside as he picked the smoldering letter out of the fire.

"Who gave you the writing supplies, Fiona?" He snarled. Blue veins rippled beneath his pale, smooth skin as he spoke.

"No one," Fiona half-sobbed. She propped herself up onto her hands and knees.

Amaranth seized her hair and dragged her across the floor to where the ink bottle's remains lay glittering in the candlelight. Broken glass and wasted ink caught at Fiona's bare arms and hands, painting her skin red and black.

"Liar," Amaranth screamed. "Liar!"

Four guards poured into the room, carrying a bound prisoner between them.

The prisoner was Thomas Denion. Thomas was a watchman from Will's class. He'd made journeyman the year before and was sent on a mission to Valeria. Sent to Valeria, but not to Amaranth's fortress. How had he fallen into the villain's hands?

Fiona howled when she saw Thomas. She scrambled to her feet and threw herself between Amaranth and the prisoner.

"No, this isn't necessary, Amaranth. I'll tell you everything. *Anything.* Please..." Frantic tears carved white lines down her smudged cheeks.

Behind her, two guards hauled a sizable trough of water in front of Thomas, while the other guards forced him to his knees.

Fiona reached out her arms in supplication. "Please, Amaranth," she whispered.

"It's too late for that, dearest. I'm afraid they won't stop dying until you stop *lying.*"

Thomas stiffened and paled.

"I don't know who sent the supplies, Amaranth," she countered. "Whoever did it wasn't stupid enough to tell me about it."

Amaranth nodded towards the guards, who began lowering Thomas's head towards the still water in the trough. Thomas wriggled and bucked against them, so that when his head went under, they all—the guards, Fiona, and Amaranth—were doused in tepid water.

Fiona rushed towards Thomas, but Amaranth caught her arm.

"You have no one to blame but yourself for this, you know," he intimated. His long-nailed fingers clawed the top fringe of her dress.

She heaved against him and spat. "Not so. You're the murderer. You kill all the watchmen your men capture for you."

"Give me something good this time, and maybe I'll spare this one."

Fiona opened her mouth, closed it. Thomas fought

underwater, but the guards had restrained him so as to reduce the excessive splashing.

"The letter," Fiona blurted out. "It was for Will. This one was for Will. There. Are you happy now?"

Amaranth curled back his lips in a slow smile. He nodded, and the guards lifted Thomas's head from the water. The boy's face was reddish-purple as he coughed and sputtered uncontrollably.

"And what did you have to say to your little Will this time?"

Fiona flicked her eyes towards Thomas, and back to Amaranth.

"What did you have to say?" He demanded, squeezing her arm.

"Don't tell him anything, my lady," Thomas rasped. "Will's my friend." One of the guards cuffed him, and he fell silent.

Fiona's eyes widened. "My Will," she mumbled. "My Will's friend."

Amaranth scowled at Thomas. "A friend of William Owain? Drowning is too good an ending for you, I think. I'll find some other way to kill you. But not today. No, we'll wait until the next time my *sweetheart* disobeys me." He pulled aside her flame-red hair and caressed her cheek.

The fire faded from Fiona's grey-green eyes. Nothing but emptiness and despair written on her beautiful features now.

"I still love him, watchman," she called to Thomas in a hollow voice. "I still care for him, no matter..."

Thomas gazed up at her solemnly. "He never forgets you, my lady. None of us from Gwynedd do."

"Take him to the lower dungeons," Amaranth snapped. "And leave us alone."

The guards dragged Thomas and the water trough from the room. Amaranth released Fiona so that he could hold the crumpled, burnt remains of the parchment to the candlelight.

She sagged to the floor.

"'Come and find me, Will'," he read in a falsetto. "What garbage. Your son is useless, Fiona. As useless as his father before him. He will never come for you. And if he does, I will find him. I will *break* him."

His gaze raked up and down Fiona's own broken figure, lingering on her face. "Oh, and you will watch every moment of it, sweetheart. Every last excruciating moment of it."

He blew out the candle.

Will could no longer make out their figures in the twilight-stricken room, but he could hear everything. Furtive scuffles and moans, and Amaranth's disgusting comments. His mother's protests, her screams, her desperate pleas. For help. For pity. For mercy.

Drip-drip-drip. Boots squeaked on slick cobblestones, mingled with the last of Fiona's anguished sobs.

Come and find me, Will.

The Fencing Tryout

Mary Rose Kreger

On the day of the Academy fencing tryouts, the summer sun drenched the Scottish Highlands with all its blue sky, untamed, melted-popsicle glory.

Philia sat in her bedroom on the second floor of her uncle's mansion, soaking in the sunlight from her window as she reviewed her list of compound fencing attacks. She'd spent most of the last two weeks in the fencing gymnasium, practicing her footwork and running drills with Dylan and Laurie. Even Uncle Haggis spared an hour to watch her fence and had given her some advice for the big day. She and Dylan had also helped his little sister Faith build her treehouse, which had been good physical training.

"Getting stronger," she sang along with the music playing on her mother's iPhone, "Getting stronger…"

"Are you listening to *Rocky?*"

Philia turned to see Laurie standing in her open doorway, dressed in a white fencing jacket and breeches. She bent her saber blade in a gentle "C" curve against the edge of her shoe.

Philia punched the air and bobbed her head in answer to Laurie's question.

"Philia Pendragon," Laurie said, shaking her head. "We should have been friends since birth."

"Yeah." Philia rose from her chair and tossed her fencing memos onto the bed. "But better late than never."

She strung up her laces to her brand-new fencing shoes; a gift from Aunt Tia when they couldn't find the right size in the warehouse. Philia whisked her fencing mask and foil blade out of the closet. She glanced in the mirror by her desk to make sure her hair was pulled back snug and then saluted Laurie.

"Right then," she said with a grin. "Are you ready to go?"

When Philia and Laurie exited the front doors of the mansion, they were greeted by the soft rolling grounds of the Knightly Academy and a sparkling sky.

"C'mon, I'll race you," Philia shouted, sprinting along as fast as she could, her fencing equipment rattling behind her. Laurie sped after her, brandishing her saber and soon passing her in a ferocious gallop. Philia stretched her legs and ran faster. Neither of them slowed until they reached the door of the gymnasium, practically plowing Dylan to the ground when he opened the door.

Whoof. The three of them landed in the grass and dirt in a jumble of arms, legs, and fencing foils. Dylan threw them off in mock anger, dusting off his shoulders and wearing an irritated expression that made the girls burst into giggles.

"Didn't your mother tell you never to run with swords?" Dylan scolded, fixing his gelled hair and flicking a piece of grass from his shirt. "We haven't even started tryouts yet and you're both out to kill me," he added under his breath.

"Oops," said Philia as she picked up her equipment and laughed at Dylan's discomfiture.

"Sorry, my boy," Laurie said. She gave him a hearty slap on the back.

"My boy?" Dylan said with a raised eyebrow, leading the way inside. "You're what, six weeks older than me?"

"Amazing how much of a difference those six weeks can make," Laurie teased.

"Miss Pendragon, you're up soon," Dylan said, smirking when Laurie rolled her eyes at him. "They're competing for advanced foil next. Laurie, my dad wanted to talk to you about the intermediate sabre team…"

Philia finished zipping up her fencing jacket and slid on her gloves. With her mask under her arm and foil in hand, she surveyed the gym to get her bearings.

She knew from Dylan's Instagram pics that her uncle had renovated the fencing gymnasium a year before. He had created a space that was both reflective of the building's Victorian past and up-to-date with modern technology. Fluorescent light fixtures and speakers hung from the tin-plated ceiling, and a new digital scoreboard had been mounted onto the original red-brick walls above metal bleachers. Three new sets of fencing platforms, or pistes, were laid out on the gym's freshly polished hardwood floors. The piste in the middle stood on a raised platform.

Prospective fencers lined up in front of each of the pistes. Philia fidgeted with her fencing gloves when she realized that the advanced foils were using the middle piste.

I guess I'll be fencing on that raised platform. Where everyone can see my every move… and my every mistake.

With trembling steps, she made her way to the tryout line for advanced foil.

"The way you've been fencing this week, you could beat at least half the members on the advanced team," Laurie had said. "Which means you have a good chance during tryouts."

So here she was, walking up to an older boy with a clipboard in his hand and a name badge that read, *Hello, I am Noah Lott.*

"Um… excuse me," Philia said, catching Noah's attention with a wave of her hand. "Is this the line for advanced foil?"

"Obviously." Noah glared down at her with a sour expression. "Your name?"

"Philia," she said, offering a tentative smile. "Philia Pendragon."

His eyes flicked down to the clipboard, back at Philia. He

looked distinctly displeased.

"Philia Pendragon," he repeated. "And how is it that the loony daughter of that crackpot author got onto our summer tryout list?"

She was taken aback by his antagonism. "I was under the impression that anyone could try out for the team," she stuttered.

"Anyone *qualified*," he retorted. "We don't want the ones that are here just because their uncle feels sorry for them."

Philia felt her blood pressure rising, but she kept her mouth shut.

"I have you for my final match," Noah continued, "and I won't be holding anything back."

She gripped her foil and glared at Noah's retreating figure.

"I won't be holding anything back, either," she muttered.

She defeated her first opponent in under two minutes, scoring 5-1. Unfortunately, her second match was against Dylan, the best fencing student in the entire Academy.

Quick as lightning, Dylan scored three points on her before she could complete a single attack. She noticed that he brought his arm up too high when he circle parried her cutovers, so she hit him twice under his fencing arm. He picked up on her strategy, and double disengaged into her left shoulder. She lured him closer with a premature lunge, then recovered forward directly into his ribs. He closed the match with a feint and strike to her right side, but by this time everyone in the gym was cheering them on. Dylan had won the match, 5-3, but at least Philia had helped give the crowd a good show.

"Excellent match, Philia," Dylan said as they shook hands. "Next time, you might beat me."

"Thank you," she said, beaming at his praise.

It wasn't long before Philia found herself mask-to-mask with Noah Lott for their final tryout match. Noah was just as good as she had expected him to be, and it took all Philia's considerable fencing knowledge and skill tied the score at 3-3.

Just two more touches to go, and I'm a free girl. She tapped her foot, wrangled Noah's fresh compound attack into an unbreakable *bind*, then flicked her foil into his chest for her fourth point.

Philia, 4. Noah, 3.

"You're dead meat, Pendragon," Noah growled through his wire mask. He shifted his feet, initiated a sloppy attack that resulted in an off-target hit to her left arm.

Philia smiled. *Time for Mum's secret weapon.*

The judge signaled for them to resume the match. Philia sprang into a horizontal leap, called a *fleche*, and slammed her foil tip neatly into Noah's chest.

"Touche!" The judge called. "Pendragon wins, 5-3."

She pulled off her mask and shook Noah and the judge's hands in a happy daze.

Noah waited for her when she descended the platform behind him.

"Where'd you learn to fence like that?" he asked with bewilderment.

"From my *mother*." Philia turned on her heel and headed to the girl's locker room, leaving Noah gaping behind her.

Mel Werner

Werner retired from Engineering and now enjoys pursuing his hobbies which include painting, gardening, weight lifting, and creative writing.

The Medallion

Mel Werner

On their way to Alpha Centauri, they stopped to investigate a small interesting planet. After three orbits of the planet, they chose several suitable landing points. The master ship would launch a three-man shuttle to explore the new world. The captain had discretion on his landing party and the landing point. Before leaving, the commander reminded him he only had the time it would take for three more orbits of the planet.

The captain chose a piece of land almost surrounded by seas. After landing, the three astronauts left the shuttle wearing their protective space suits. The first thing the captain did was read his spectrometer: nitrogen and oxygen with an assortment of other gases. The air was breathable, very similar to home. They removed their helmets and took deep breaths. The air was fresh.

This green world had no life except for plants and insects. A sample of the liquid showed it to be two parts hydrogen and one part oxygen; the purest natural water they had ever encountered. He broke the rules when he removed his gloves and dipped a finger in the water. Then the captain rubbed his finger to his thumb. The cool liquid felt wet and slippery. He smelled it and was very tempted to taste it, but resisted. He looked at the green hills and the beautiful sky; this was paradise.

The three crewmen made their way from the sandy beach through thick vegetation. After a long hike they came to a clearing. Mixed with plant life they found rocks and rubble. Then they made their first significant discovery. Behind thick bushes was a small, isolated wall with a doorway. The captain ducked through the short opening. On the other side was more vegetation, but clearly this wall was not a natural phenomenon; it had a design. Stones in the wall were equal in size with a mortar-like substance holding them together. There had been intelligent beings living here. The beings were long gone; from the lack of ruins, it appeared to have been many thousands of years ago.

The captain's specialty was anthropology. The female in his landing crew was a botanist and the other male was the pilot of their shuttle. Checking his instruments again indicated slight radiation. He then calculated its half life. Calculations pointed to a very high radioactive level ten thousand years ago. Was this the reason for the extinction of this lost race? In his studies he had learned there could be many reasons; plagues, seismic activity, collisions with large meteors, even war. It would take years of study to discover a reason and they were visiting for only a short time. The truth was it could be something as simple as lack of oxygen even though twenty-one percent was perfect for him.

Searching the rubble around the wall he made an extraordinary find. He reached down and picked-up a small round disk. Between his fingers he rubbed it clean. Flipping it over revealed images on both sides. This was the most significant discovery they had made in their very long mission. On one side was a profile of an alien being. The being had a nose at the center of his face, much more pronounced than his own. Assuming the profile was symmetrical, there were two eyes. Also, there were protrusions on the sides of its head and under its nostrils was a very large mouth-like opening. There was a fur-like covering on top of its head, and it wrapped around under it. The being was clothed, but its clothing was folded and wrinkled, unlike his own synthetic clothing.

On the reverse side was a dwelling. He put his helmet back on, then he flipped his magnifying visor down; oops, wrong one. This one was used for distance. He flipped the other one down. There it was, a being was seated in the dwelling. Rolling the medallion over again he studied the being with his magnifier. Under its shoulder he discovered a very small symbol; it read, VDB. He wondered why the text was so small. All of the other symbols were easy to read, although they had no meaning; 1994, In God We Trust, One Cent, United States of America, E. Pluribus Unum.

Back on the master ship, they would enter the symbols on their computer, although without additional information, he feared there would be no breakthrough. Putting the disk into his instrumentation, a light passed over it: mass 63.5, metal with cubic crystal structure, indicating copper with other trace metals.

The anthropologist folded his three long ash gray fingers around the disk and carried it to his collection case. Securing it inside the case, he then made his way back to the finding place. Then his communicator beeped three times; it was the commander announcing it was time to return to the orbiting ship. Asking the commander for more time, the request was denied. Another orbit would put the ship too far from the shuttle.

He called out to his crew members. "Meorg togha vindabose (we have orders to leave)." The female walked over and faced him. They were able to telecommunicate, but only when they were face to face. She transferred her thoughts, "Jabin vindabose tootie (Must we leave already)?"

The captain looked into her large almond-shaped eyes, they were a very rare violet color. "Juta leda furbros (Our commander insists)."

The pilot spoke; "Leda soci mea moday (Commander is the boss)."

They gathered their equipment and findings, took quick recordings of the doorway and hiked back to the beach. The botanist entered the shuttle first. She was petite for a female; the captain estimated barely two meters tall. It felt a little awkward, him being taller than this female, but those eyes more than made up for it. Then the pilot entered and took his place at the controls.

Before the captain entered the craft, it started to rain. On his home planet he had only experienced rain a dozen times in his almost two hundred years

"Trotin shera ja carmona (This planet has everything)."

The reason for their mission was to find suitable planets to colonize. In his opinion this one was a prime candidate. He'd love to be one of the pilgrims and live in this wonderful place. Its radiation was a problem, but in less than one thousand years, it would be completely safe. The problem was in a thousand years he would be quite old and not suitable for the adventure. He thought maybe his offspring, or theirs, could return.

Offspring? It was time to get serious about reproducing. Most associates his age had one or two already.

He'd have to pick a mate. Maybe the female botanist in his landing party. He detected her rising pheromones. Also his body temperature went up a full centigrade when near her. Both were good mating signs. He preferred a physical mating rather than lab created offspring, much like his parents when they bore him almost two centuries ago.

When he confided with his closest shipmates, they were repulsed. "That was the way the primitives reproduced thousands of years ago. If you need sexual gratification, take a pill."

The crew was evenly divided with twelve females and twelve males. It was important since the duration of their exploration was fifty years.

There was a problem, the female botanist was admired by their commander, but he was almost three times her age. When next to him, there was no increase in pheromones. Still, the commander had the status of rank.

The shuttle returned to the master ship, and they left orbit. He removed his space suit and decontaminated in the ultraviolet light room. Then the captain changed into his on board uniform. He looked out toward the planet. The shrinking blue sphere filled his view port. He saw his landing site located in the northern hemisphere. It was centered in a huge land mass. Its distinctive shape was surrounded on three sides by great lakes of different sizes.

What catastrophe had befallen these people? What robbed them of the opportunity to live in such a wonderful world? The answers would have to wait for another visit, another day.

Today he was hungry, so he made his way to the nutrition room. After grabbing a palette and passing it under the dispensing unit, an array of colored plant based-paste was arranged on it. Then he searched the room for a place to ingest his meal. Standing by a small table was the female botanist; he walked over to her. She lowered her palette after she gracefully licked one of the lines of paste off of it.

"Troden seena mybin fora chey (1231, mind if I join you)?"

She nodded her approval and smiled with her beautiful almond-shaped eyes.

Siete 16 Guevara

Siete16 Guevara. Mexican American. Son. Brother. Husband. Father. Poet. Born and bred in Michigan. Was a Texan from the Rio Grande Valley. Siete16 published three books of his own poetry, and is working on the fourth book. Siete16 writes and speaks passionately about his belief of Familia, Community and Raza; what he sees and describes as being good or bad; and what he wants to bring to light for others to see.

Siete16 is the Artistic/Creative Director for Artistas Latinx en Acción Siempre (A.L.A.S.). This non-profit organization works on building communities and networks with other Latinx/Hispanic Artists to work together, support each other, perform together in their communities or go where the "Gringos" are and entertain them. He is actively involved in several writing collectives in his area of Sterling Heights and Warren. His books are currently in eight libraries in Michigan. His goal is getting more of his books into ALL Michigan Libraries.

RAIN and TEARS
Inspired by Esmer of RGV, TX

Siete 16 Guevara

Rain Tears Rain Tears Rain Tears

Rain **Rain falls on me and** Tears

Rain **cleanses me of the** Tears

Rain **filth and my guilt.** Tears

Rain **that I carry on me** Tears

Rain Tears Rain Tears Rain Tears

Rain **While Tears from my** Tears

Rain **eyes cleanse my** Tears

Rain **Heart and Soul** Tears

Rain **of the Sins and Pain** Tears

Rain Tears Rain Tears Rain Tears

I hear thunder in the distance,

A rainstorm is coming.

I go out there to embrace it.

Rain Tears Rain Tears Rain Tears

No one notices your Tears in the Rain.

Don't Forget Me

Siete 16 Guevara

Day of the Dead
is when we remember
Those we love and lost in
during Our Life –
and We feel empty because they
are Gone –
and We miss Them.

During these
Three Days – the beginning of November
We celebrate their lives.
With food, music, dancing and laughter.
We share pictures of them,
Stories about them,
And We remember them.

As long as we are here,

Their Descendants –

Su Familia –

Los Muertos

They are not truly gone and

They are not forgotten.

They come home to visit

from where they rest and dwell

crossing over a bridge that is created by Marigold petals

and lead by glowing Candles to show them

the way Home.

Los Muertos and Their Descendants –

Familia Conjuntos –

Walking around singing, dancing, laughing and

having FUN!

BUT

Most Importantly –

Nos Recordamos Los

We Don't Forget THEM.

Ghazwan Saaid

Born in Iraq. after many years working as an architect, he started a humanitarian organization to work among refugees and displaced people in Iraq, who were victims of the religious and sectarian conflict. This is where he started to see the world in a different way.

He studied theology, eastern culture and wrote books in Arabic and English, novels and articles all about how to understand and accept people who are different. In 2014, after ISIS invaded Iraq and Syria, he escaped death with his family and fled the country coming to live in the United States of America. He enjoys attending the creative writers workshop in Sterling Heights where he lives, and where his son and daughter attend schools. He doesn't mind the snowy cold weather in Michigan as long as there are people to read his stories.

Mail of a Different Kind

Ghazwan Saaid

In vain I was trying to keep it alive inside me, the country, where I was born. I surrounded myself with old memories, pictures from the past reminding me of the people whom I knew there. Repeating their names, following them on Facebook and other social media; that was my consolation in coffee-time during the day. I listened to my country's songs while preparing an old authentic meal, the meal my mother used to cook for me. Trying hard to cling to the love of my homeland as a solemn and sincere person; holding out against many years of alienation. Not a day went by without thinking of the land that embraced me, embraced my ancestors and cuddling their graves.

Suddenly, a sound of a rattling engine raided my world. I jolted, glanced at the watch, perceptive of the hazard and aware of who it was. As the forthcoming person drew near, a wave of fear and dread swept over my body. Yes, it's her. I can hear the footfalls; here she comes in the same timing of every day. She never missed a day or was late once. Holding my breath, I listened to the sound of the box door. It squeaked open for a while then let go, fell and closed. I took a deep sigh of breath, hoping that the mailbox was her only task for today and she will turn around and leave, so will the potential intimidation. But a thrilling sound of footsteps kept approaching the threshold. Then the doorbell rang; I flinched and clutched to my seat unwilling to obey the reiterated calls recalling insistently. Eventually, I headed for the door submissive.

A broad smile the size of the horizon overlooked onto my trepidations once I opened the door. She greeted me, "How are you sir," stretched her shapely hand, and handed me the certified mail she couldn't drop in the box.

Hypnotized, driven by her greeting, I grabbed the letters and took a long look at them. Letters from people in different states who cared about me and my needs. An act of love!

Has anyone loved me back home? Has anyone been there to take care of my needs?

No one had ever brought me mail! They never cared about me.

She said pointing to a record in her hand, "May I have your signature here, please."

I looked straight at her face, overwhelmed by her smile, recalling myself. People working in public services back home never smiled that way; they were always upset. And definitely, they didn't have such marvelous blue eyes like hers.

She repeated, "Your signature, sir!"

I grasped the pen and scratched my name's letters in English; I found my name's shape more beautiful than before. I sealed the bottom of the paper, approving this reality which I kept avoiding, admitting to the fact of this better life.

"Thank you, sir. Have a good day," she said.

Before she turned back, I clapped the door in her face. As if I was ending the heavy storm that wiped away the tangled remains of my home country out of my head. I spun around seeking to clutch something, a thing that has a substantial impact. More than the picture or a name or the text messages. A real implement of defense against that devastating storm that made all my previous daily tools useless. I ran towards the bedroom, climbed the stairs to the upper story. "*Hurry up*," I said to myself, "*quickly*," before losing the last string connecting me to my homeland; already its blurry features were vanishing from my head.

I unfolded the closet searching, and then pulled the suitcase I brought with me when I came to this country ten years ago. Unzipping it wide open; I tucked my head inside and deeply inhaled filling my lungs. I breathed and breathed as if I was breathing the scent of life. I sighed relieved for regaining the smell and restoring my country stored in that case I kept for such a day. The day I stand powerless confronting my present reality. I passed my fingers along the bag, feeling its fabric. Recalling my life before ten years ago when I left my country.

Details of the traveling day still engraved in my memory, the faces, and pictures. The gloomy features of the porters, frowning weary under the heavyweight of the bag, murmuring together, unwilling to engage in a conversation with me. I can still feel their hands all over the bag to the handle. I touched the Cross, fixed to the handle and recalled how much I was worried when my mother tied this Cross there; it was big, colored and eye-catching. She said it would help me distinguish it among other bags of the same size and shape. I knew she just wanted to send something belonging to her with me, something to protect me. But that cross confused me at the airport that day; I was scared of everyone around me, most of all, scared of the extremist Islamists, and the possibility of being targeted by them because of that cross. They would be agitated furiously by it. I loved that cross, though, as my family did. It's our emblem and core of faith, the same time was the cause for our persecution in that country.

I passed my fingers to the side pocket of the bag and felt something inside; I don't remember putting something there! I tucked my hand deep, and I was surprised! It was a letter! But I kept all my valued papers with my passport in my handbag, which I carried alongside with my laptop onto the plane. I unfolded the letter; a hard shock swept me when my eyes read the written line, *"Get out of our country, you infidel."*

Dryness

Ghazwan Saaid

The roaring sound of the garage door motor awoke her to life from the full obscurity that often overtook her during the day. The persistent reflections from the past swept her far beyond reality. Settled in her seat, glued to the couch and her feet stretched—that's how she used to spend mid afternoons. The cell phone in her hand was her only link to the outside world. She opened her eyes and glanced ahead at the clock fixed on the wall, then turned her sight to the door which was opening slowly.

Once the door opened, he stepped into the house, humming a song, and tossed the school bag on the floor, then he took off his coat and threw it on a chair beside the dining table. He turned to her with a face full of serenity, smiled, and said, "Hi Mom, how are you?" He stepped forward to where she was laying and folded his arms around her, longing for the generous love she never provided for him. She stood silent and gave him a long stare, like a rock, without moving a limb.

"What is it?" he asked, but she didn't answer. He straightened in his seat and asked again, "Is there something wrong?"

"Yes," she replied in a low voice. "Today, I logged into the PowerSchool. Your grades are dropping!" She paused for a while, struggling to make her voice calm, then asked with eyes full of reproach and blame, "Have you been doing your homework?"

He threw her a gaze of irritation and replied, "I've told you many times that there's no need to remind me of my homework. I am a grown boy now and know when to do it."

She interrupted him. "Then why did your grades go down?"

"I told you, I know what I am doing," he said, and reminded her: "Mom, don't forget that we are not living in Iraq anymore! This is America." He paused for a while then stated in a definite voice, "You have the right to question me at the end of the semester."

In a sharp tone, she said, "Your semester grades won't be good enough if you don't study and do your best. That is why I am so concerned and always worried about you." Her voice became much louder. "Can't you see how anxious you are making me?"

He sighed heavily and lowered his head. Then he stood up without saying a word and headed to the upper floor and his room. After all these years with her, he had learned not to go any farther with these discussions. He had to accept everything she said. No matter the result, she wouldn't be satisfied by the profound insight of a young boy like him, a truth she couldn't realize in spite of the fact that he was a man now, though he had proved himself in front of her many times before. He was already in high school, and next month he would get his driver's license. He couldn't stop the flowing anxiety nested in her heart.

She watched him strolling out of the living room, unable to understand how he could act calmly amid such a furious situation, at least it was a furious situation for her. His way of life featured a slow and soft rhythm, despite the hard childhood he had lived in the first ten years of his life, which were permeated by war and conflict in the country where he was born. From those early years, he went through many devastating experiences and witnessed several wars in a country controlled by fire and bullets. He had to flee with her and abandon home repeatedly, seeking safe places, and spending nights with her in underground shelters, escaping all kinds of bombs launched by the warplanes or carried on missiles from overseas.

He was taught by his father where and how to position himself if there was a shooting or aerial bombardment nearby. She can't forget the first time they made him place the gas mask on his head—a big, black rubber mask, with two glass openings in the front. He didn't complain though; as a baby, he was excited and thought it was a game. She panicked at this scene and thought he would die, so she couldn't stop herself from crying. She cried a lot that day.

His life was soaked with bullets, air bombardments, and car bombs. Doors used to fly off from their thresholds; shattering glass and broken windows spread around him while he was playing with his Teddy bear. In the nights, he slept through the falling sounds of faraway battles, but he perfectly handled all these effects, and controlled its collisions on his soul, and succeeded in not letting it dominate his personality and future. He prevented that severe history from inhabiting his life forever and overcame it in a consistent, smart way, domesticating all the effective reactions and maladies planted in his early childhood.

Such pain and psychological impact were as big as a mountain for a young boy like him; the heavyweight was enough to crush the shoulders of a grown man, but he learned from his early years how to develop and invent specific ways to endure that burden. Despite all the circumstances surrounding him, he grasped the fact that a human being must survive, struggle, fight back, and sometimes create new ideas just to stay alive. Simply put, he was a result of wars and conflicts. Yet, the outcome was a smart boy who had conquered the obstacles forced upon him and had chosen his own way in life out of his painful and unfair reality.

She was still pinned to the couch, yet her eyes followed him as he disappeared into the hallway. Quiet and sad, she was incapable of managing these fears and worries that emerged from her past life. Everything consumed her, and everything had been forced upon her until all that fear and anxiety became rooted deeply inside, unwilling to go away even after all these years. Now the causative disappeared from her life after she left her country, but she couldn't erase the images of all that running and hiding, the persistent quest to seek a safe refuge for the family, for her only son. It was a heavy burden that she had carried on her shoulders for long time.

She couldn't deny the many years of suppression, fears, insults, and the misery of a country that didn't respect her as a human being. For sure, the past never passes away! The places would change, and she would become older or even adopt a new career, but the past wouldn't leave her in peace, it was as if it dug deep into her life. Like a dominant oil company spending a long time searching for a specific piece of land and bought later, then drilled a long heavy pipe that went hundreds of feet deep inside that property. That long pipe would not be removed easily, no matter how much that land or its neighbors desired and tried to take it out. It wouldn't be removed unless the company consumed all it needed and until that land was drained of its resources and became deserted; so was she captured and possessed, precisely like that piece of land. The remains of the past denied her being set free, clutched her firmly, stripping her of ordinary life so she missed being like other normal people. She was dry after all these events took everything from her; there were no tears to shed if she ought to cry!

She tangled her fingers together, holding herself, making sure not to scatter on the ground; choking and trying hard to gasp breaths. She drew a long breath; it came intermittently, like the sound of bullets coming out of an automatic gun. It was the same sound she used to hear coming from the streets back in the homeland. She quickly cupped her hands over her mouth and struggled to stifle the gathering cry before it came out so that he wouldn't hear her wailing again. Enough of being the bothersome mother to him.

When he heard her suppressed wailing, he paused on his way to the stairs, turned back to the living room, hugged her, and said to calm her down, "Don't be afraid, Mom. Everything will be alright. There's no need to worry." He looked at her face with overwhelming love. "Enough of being scared. We are safe now; nobody can harm us here." Then he pulled her hands up to his mouth and kissed them. She was staring at him. His eyes were shining with great hope when he said, "Stop worrying about me. I am doing fine; at least I am still alive, enjoying a normal life in this country."

With a smile of trust covering his face, he declared, "Here, I enjoy doing things I couldn't do before like growing and decorating my hair." He pointed to his hair. "I can brush it, dye it, and form it as I wish. Do you remember how back home I was afraid to grow it longer? I was deprived of doing what I wished. Boys who did things like this were either kidnapped or killed. Mom, that hard country tried to deprive me of my childhood. But now I am free, Look! See how long and handsome my hair is now!" He leaned back, pulling up his chestnut curls which shined beautifully under the sunbeams coming from the window.

Incapable of moving a hand, she glanced at his hair and said, "And your hair is the reason you are always late for the school bus early morning; because of spending a long time taking care of it, more than doing your homework. I wish I could cut it for you."

"No way, that will not happen," he opposed, "all but except my hair. I am now like Samson the Great; my strength comes from my hair." He looked at her scoffing, "Without my hair, I won't be able to get high grades in school. Most important of all, without my hair, I won't be able to make you laugh when you get sad as you are now." He stood, tilted his front hair to the left and right, waving his front hair up in the air. He looked like a crazy parrot with fluffy feathers; this made her rejoice, and she laughed at the scene. He laughed, too.

Looking at him, she wondered how the way he laughed hadn't changed at all even though he had grown and become a big boy. As if he was the same three-year-old child whose giggles filled the world with joy and swept away all the sadness and gloominess dominating her life. She recalled the night when the war started. That night the first wave of missiles was launched by the American forces, targeting a security compound that was close to their house. That compound was controlled by Saddam Hussein's regime, during the Gulf War in 1990.

She remembered how much she hated that compound and wished it to be demolished. It was highly protected and surrounded by dozens of armed men cloaked in black. Should anyone approach it, they could be killed. The scene of the high grey concrete walls made her heart beats speed up, and fear would emerge throughout her body whenever she passed it on her way back from work. There were a lot of horrifying stories about the place and how the guardians treated the prisoners. A lot of people who had been admitted there did not come out alive.

That night, the entire zone had been blocked including their neighborhood. Because of the war alert, nobody could go in or come out, so they had no other choice but to stay home and hope they would be safe. She was holding him in her arms as they both clung to the corner of the bedroom, waiting and counting the passing minutes. She was praying to survive that hard night when the first cruise missile cut the sky on its way down to its target. The speeding missile made a high, squeaky sound before striking the earth and exploding.

He looked at her and burst out laughing at that heavy wheezing. Despite the rattling sound of the explosion, he kept laughing and laughing with each missile breaking through the air. Ten rockets and ten blasts carried enough destructive power to bring a whole city to the ground, wipe away all houses and kill thousands of people, and he was laughing! All the fear vanished in front of his loud, innocent giggles filling the room and turning that horrible situation into a tolerable state.

At first, she couldn't comprehend how he could be laughing. However, she laughed with him, for once, reckless of that hard situation and all the terrifying sounds surrounding them. He had turned fear and death into a funny, creative moment. From childhood, he had been able to adapt to his surroundings. No matter how unfortunate his reality was, he would turn it into something good, also motivating others to see life differently, in a way that boosts more meaning to life, more hope and prospect. She smiled and said, "You are," paused and took a longing look at him then released her hands slowly, hugged him, let out a long sigh and added, "My Home." A tear like a pearl was all she had at that moment, it fell to the ground.

In The Lost Time

Ghazwan Saaid

Loud rattling sounds woke me up early in the morning. I flipped in my bed many times, desperately trying to sleep again. Sounds of hammering kept pounding insistently. No way I could go back to sleep. Finally, I opened my eyes subjected to the role of this noise, as I am subjected to many things in my life. That was my mornings for the past week because of the construction across the street, in the new subdivision where I lived one year after I came.

I went down to my office and sat on the chair in front of the big high window. That window overlooked the front yard, close to the street and the new houses being built across it, from which all that annoying sound have been coming. I opened the laptop, snapped the power key and went browsing through my emails. I paused at a past email from Terry of the creative writers workshop in Sterling Heights Library. "Hello writers," she would be addressing us, "Bring your work for some critic... at our meeting 6 pm on Tuesday... happy writing, Terry." I glanced at the corner of the screen and saw the date; today is Tuesday. It was the day of the meeting! I always longed for that meeting, but to attend it, I had to write something. I headed to the kitchen to brew some coffee and prepare myself for the mission impossible. I grasped my cup then retreated to the office and resettled in my place. I sighed briefly facing the keyboard.

This time I must write a piece without any misspellings or grammar mistakes. This time I need to elaborate my language. English was not my mother tongue, so nailing the story and putting it in a perfect parlance was a hard task for an immigrant like me who merely spent three years in this country. It made my life hard as a writer.

The voices of the workers outside rose higher; I looked through my giant window. The scene grabbed my attention. Four men were working on the brick wall, building it into the front elevation of a colonial house. An old man with broad shoulders behaved like a master of this crew. He was the one to choose the bricks and install them on the desired spot of the wall as he had the required expertise for such kind of job. The rest were assistants. The close one was handing his master the requested brick. The other one prepared the cement required as an adhesive for fixing the bricks together on that wall, flipping it over with a shovel so that it won't dry and become useless. A younger man and the last was holding a wooden broom in his hands, cleaning the surroundings. A typical scene for a construction building crew, but for this team, it won't be perfect for them without an audio sound recorder playing, in a high volume, with an unpleasant voice singer shouting in a Latin song. I had no desire to listen to a song which I couldn't get a clue of what it was about! Unlike me, the workers looked pretty acquainted, though fully engaged in their task. Working with their hands was a hard-physical job, so they needed something as an escape, just to fill their heads, till they finished their weary day. Their life as workers looked hard.

Back to my laptop, I wrote in the middle of the page "life is too hard." Writing about how hard life could be was a good subject for today's meeting. I bet other writers would like it! People always loved to read exciting stories and hear about the hard life of others. Though, hard life, in fact, was so simple. Hard life was always flat. Most of the times it was dull, harsh, like the life of these hard-working laborers. Harsh and flat that was my definition of a hard life. Suddenly, the young man with the broom went on dancing, swayed his body and shuffled his feet, embracing the broom in his hands. As if he had a girl, he was spinning around with the broom, like a couple on a stage dancing the waltz. The others paused and watched him astonished, then one of them cheered and acclaimed in Spanish, the other pointed to the dancing worker, a signal like he was a crazy person. They all laughed at his scene. While he was holding, with passion, the wooden broom, his face beamed with happiness. When he lifted his head facing the sky with closed eyes, he revived like he had a beautiful girl hanging in his hands, swirling as an angel on the beats of that ugly voice of the deserted singer.

This scene lasted for seconds before the master yelled at them, and they all went back to work. They just wanted to finish their job and go home. Submissive to their reality; there was no place for entertainment or enjoyment. The young man looked at them nonchalantly for their mocking; he finished his dance though, then went back to work, laughing with an open mouth, full of happiness and joy. He didn't have to carry his burden in a dispiriting way, such a passive way. He wanted to make his hard job flourishing and easy. The shining sun on his beaming face with his eyes closed reminded me of how capable a human being is of fighting back his hard life, and creating lightness and freshness for his life, even when he is under hard conditions. Such a situation fully imposed in his life. However, he can see things differently. He has the power to create a happy zone, a contented state, for him and others. Overcoming hardness and oppression demands a throbbing heart which beats strongly with hope to rise and stand up motivated, to dance in the hardest and exhausting situations, that any person could ever have.

I looked at the clock; it was 4 pm. It's amazing how time

passed fast on me! I spent my day watching these workers, and I missed writing any words except the title, "Life Is Too Hard." I thought maybe there is still a chance to write a short story before the workshop starts. I did the calculating, ten minutes to change my clothes. Then to save some time to get to the library at the city of Sterling Heights, I had to pass Hall Road, due to all the construction work going on there, and go through the residential area by Dodge Park road this way I can make it in twenty minutes.

That leaves me with only ninety minutes to think of a good plot, write it down, revise and print it out. The face of Terry popped up in front of me, smiling, surrounded by the other writers, waiting for my story; they were all longing to perform some critique. I will need more than ninety minutes to write such a subject in English, it was embarrassing when I shared my work, full of all these language mistakes. Sometimes I looked funny, crazy, for just doing that. The thoughts kept circling in my head while the ninety minutes were shrinking. Time was passing in steps, accelerating like a rabbit running into some green meadows leaving his trail only, a spot no more. Hard! It's too hard. My head heated with thoughts and ideas, pictures and people's faces tangled all together.

I looked out the window; the workers were preparing to go home after they finished their day job. I breathed a deep sigh of relief and looked at the screen. "Life Is Too Hard." I glanced at the clock. I was in the lost time. I snapped the keyboard and wrote four words to complete the story; then hit the "print" icon. The machine started juddering.

I turned off the laptop and held my keys. Stretched my hand and grabbed the papers out of the printer, then turned around to leave. I smiled when I stepped out of the door and said, "Life is too hard; be easy into it."

Sarah Lynne John

Sarah John is a former technical writing and communications professional, who has become a stay-at-home mom. Now that she has successfully shipped her kids off to school, creative writing is finding its way back into her life and onto the page. She has always been a traveler and adventure-seeker; sky-diving over Oahu, sampling escargot in Paris, cliff jumping in Utah, para-gliding in the Alps, and even eating fruitcake in Siberia. She has found a true outlet for life's experiences in crafting stories and translating powerful emotions into poetry.

Beautiful Creatures

Sarah Lynne John

In this room, all is quiet, all is still;
My head, I lay down on the windowsill.
Radiant ribbons of light warm my skin.
I, a statue, full of motion within.

Each second, each day my heart does contract,
Oxygen, nutrients, hormones, all packed,
The liquid of life, sent on its way.
Ninety thousand miles. Go, without delay.

Each hour ten million red blood cells bred.
Fifty thousand skin cells, each minute shed.
Cell to cell circuits to think and to store,
To react, to learn and love evermore.

Firing neurons warn me, when it's too much,
Circles of ridges enhance fingers' touch—
One hundred times more, sensing vibration,
Spotting gradation, sharing affection

Flexing and stretching, taut muscle and bone.
Seventeen to grin, forty-three to moan:
Joy is inherent. Depression, be gone!
Explosions of motion—Jump and catch on!

It's true. We are all beautiful creatures,
Every One: unique strengths, gifts and features,
Exquisitely crafted by Him who cares
In His image to house God's cherished heirs.

The Inconvenience of Perfection

Sarah Lynne John

It isn't always convenient to be married to a man like my husband. I have endured many a social gathering of women in silence where I can't contribute to the marital complaints being shared. Somehow describing his dedication to me and our family never goes over well in this setting. These women don't want to hear how he chooses to fill his life with date nights, homework help and family vacations, over boy nights, video games and fishing trips. Nor do they want to hear about his exceptional work ethic and total selflessness.

For him, it goes beyond "helping around the house." He takes ownership of the responsibility, and occasionally I have to stop him from doing the children's chores as well. How does he think they will learn to contribute to our family if he folds their laundry and empties the dishwasher for them? If, after a long day at work, I ask him to cook dinner, he accepts the challenge with gusto, whipping up hamburgers and milkshakes or Belgian waffles. My "honey-do" lists never have a long lifespan, and I actually have to coax him away from household tasks to sit on the couch in the evening and watch a show with me.

Along with hampering my girlfriend commiserations, it is certainly inconvenient to wait while he does the "considerate" thing, such as letting people go ahead of us in traffic jams, picking up garbage at the park, or re-shelving an item at the grocery store in its proper place, even though we are on the opposite side of the store when I decide we don't need it.

It goes beyond inconvenience when, despite their protests, you begin to see your own traitorous parents and siblings come to love and admire the man you married more than their own daughter and sister!

It is not my fault that I was lured into this marriage by his tan, bulging biceps. I was young! I can hardly be blamed that he makes me feel like the center of the universe, even twenty years later. His humor and enthusiasm for life are as dazzling as his kindness and compassion.

I've come to realize that I just have to put up with these inconveniences in life. After all, nobody is perfect, or so they say.

C$_2$H$_6$O

Sarah Lynne John

You killed my cousin on the road,
   Crossed the line, your weapon flew.
Your wasted partner—overload;
   Gone his passions, worries too.

You damaged brain cells in the womb;
   Made my daughter's future dim.
She, who bore her, chose to consume.
   Innocent babes—You strike at whim.

You punched a hole right through my home:
   Driver splayed on cement floor;
Shattered glass; angry, tangled chrome.
   Refuge breached without the door.

You robbed me of my sister's life.

Wretched, evil substance, Die!

She tried to hide her inner strife.

Thirty-two, a mother. Why!?

Your tendrils wove within her brain,

Driving need for dopamine.

Your subtle tactics forged a chain,

Spirit broken—not foreseen.

How many ways do you destroy?

Can't the world see through your lies?

Addictive pleasures stamp out joy.

My heart splinters—Hear my cries!

Cynthia Anne Hurt

Cynthia Anne Hurt (CrowCAH) is currently editing her first full-length novel. A pirate swashbuckler at heart, CrowCAH pillages the keyboard to write her novels, novellas, short stories, and poetry, while plundering the bookshelves for reading material.

She is a member of the Sterling Heights Public Library Creative Writers Workshop, Romance Writers of America and local Greater Detroit chapter, and the Tuesday Morning Writers. Hurt has been a lifelong resident of Sterling Heights, Michigan. Contact her at cynthiaannehurt@gmail.com.

The Challenge

Cynthia Anne Hurt

The Wailing Sirens sang out in the Sol Phairian, guardian angel atmosphere.

Keegan startled, groaned, and glanced at the clock; it read 8 AM. Turning over, he saw the usual pale blue sky was an unnatural slate gray. Worried, he fastened the stainless-steel gladiator uniform over his massive shoulders, buckling the straps between his large opal tinged wings, and draped a blood red cloak down his back.

"It better not be those pyrates, again, asking for admittance." He rubbed the pantheon Phoenix crest on his chest, for continued fortitude.

A knock thundered at the door. "Leader, are you awake?" shouted Lieutenant Grunnell. "It's the Sol Phalians, they've broken the border."

Keegan scowled. He found four of his squadron, all dressed like him, waiting for his command. "To the Pegasi, we ride."

They flew the distance, getting to the stable just as the animals were being harnessed to the chariots.

The winged horses were prancing and neighing their displeasure at being disturbed.

With a flick of the soldier's silver whips, they rode into the gloomy sky.

Keegan could make out a line of Sol Phalian riders, a mile

distant, just within the Light protected wall border. Why didn't they sack the city while they had the chance? Why did they stop? Pulling up in front of their leader, who waited with his Dragoons, Keegan signaled for his Warriors to halt.

The Phalian Dragohorses spewed fire balls, engulfing the dimmed atmosphere with an eerie luminescence.

"Who dare defy," Keegan challenged, "the sacred Sol Phairian Lighted border with their Darkness?"

The Leader smiled showing sharp yellowed teeth. "I am Rohirrim, Master of the Sol Phalian Storm Guard." He was resplendent in a thorny hematite breast plate, mirroring his sallow skin and angular face.

"Keegan, Leader of the Sol Phairian Warriors," he saluted, bowing, and pounding a fist to his chest.

"I have a message from my king, King Rothfuss. The Power is growing and even you can't save them all."

"What?"

"It's already started. We broke through your walls," Rohirrim said, with a sweep of his hand. "We can gain access anywhere."

"Be gone with you. Tell your King to protect his own."

"But, Keegan, that is your name? Descendant of the Fiery One? You are one of His own. Give in to your true nature. Join us. Let us show you how to use the Power."

"Enough. I will not join you, rogue of the air. I am a Sol Phairian." Keegan turned his Pegasus' head towards home.

"Was it always that way, Warrior? How else do you think you got that title?"

"I earned it by my strength and protecting the citizens of Cloud Nine," Keegan threw over his shoulder.

"Ha! Not all Angels are given such strength and speed. You learned to be compassionate. It's against your nature. Come back to us. Come home. The Power cannot wait forever. It prefers you make the choice willingly, but it will force your wings if it has to."

Turning to face his adversary, Keegan spat, "The Light will prevail over Darkness."

"Suit yourself. I would like us to be comrades. Not sworn enemies. But if you prefer it..." Rohirrim raised his hand and snapped his fingers. A flash of purple lightning fissured, igniting Keegan's chariot. From the clouds erupted a deep-throated growl.

"You forgot I could fly." Keegan leapt off the burning conveyance, slashed the Pegasus' yoke, and darted forwards. His broad sword zinged through the atmosphere, reverberating against his opponent's spiked shield.

Rohirrim rotated the shield but was unable to wrench the weapon out of Keegan's hands.

Yanking the sword back, Keegan failed another attempt to penetrate the enemy's thorny armor. He hovered, waiting for the attack and glaring. "Fight me, you coward."

"I thought we were, Warrior," his adversary taunted. He snapped again, a white lightning bolt appeared in his hand, and, with a flick of his wrist, he hurled it.

"Cheat," Keegan roared, wings still beating the air, burning his hands as he tried to pull the bolt free from his heart.

"Dust to dust, ashes to ashes." Rohirrim grinned and turned his dragohorse. "The Power will be back for you." He flew into the mist, taking his Dragoons and the black clouds with him.

Once more, the sun shone bright and clear. Keegan lifted his head to it but could not smile at its beauty or warmth. He knew the consequences of losing.

His wings ceased to beat as he fell from the Heavens. His wings erupted into flame, charred black, and dissolved. They sprouted back dull gray with one black feather.

He had become a Fallen.

Behind Closed Doors

Cynthia Anne Hurt

Come, open the door.
I obeyed and soon heard
A merry mermaid singing

Water all around her
Variety found in vast oceans
Salty teeming with life

She greeted with a smile
Of her guile I did ignore
Swimming out to her boulder

She allowed me to sit
Join in her repast
Bountiful delicious delicacies

Feverishly I ate my fill
Excusing my parched lips
I drank more readily of her beauty

Satisfied at leisure
Her sisters came in bounds
To investigate an old friend

I lay dumbstruck
A leech for their caresses
Sweet sounding songs

Nothing more do I require
Than to lay back down
No longer under their spell

For when I do wake
These creatures will be no more
A mirage in my memory

Now I'm at rest and peace
Slumbering as I do every night
Safely behind closed lid's door

Greg Schindler

A native of Center Line and graduate of EMU, Schindler lived in San Francisco and New York during the seventies, then returned to southeastern Michigan.

He's a long time poet, working more in prose recently. He likes to think the quality of his prose is approaching that of his poetry.

E-I-E-I-OINK

Greg Schindler

My lady bird flew the coop today,
A homing pigeon, to her parents.
"Good week!"
She tweeted on the tarmac.
"Good trip!" I wished back.
Twixt airport and home
Meijer's allure reeled me in.
I turtle-crawled the aisles,
A wise owl eyeing labels.
An odd item hopped into my cart
Then multiplied quite rabbitish.
Like stray puppies
They followed me home
Where I squirreled them away
Greedy as a packrat.
So now I graze.
Soooome pig.

Rena Davis

Rena Davis, retired Army Sergeant, is a short story author, editor, blogger, and novelist. Currently, she is working on a young adult fantasy series and an action based short story collection.

She is a member of the Tuesday Morning Writers and an active participant in the Sterling Heights Creative Writers Workshop.

Visit BookHavenMagazine.com

Army Strong

Rena Davis

"Not this shit again," I growled, checking the clock. 2350. What the hell! I fell asleep thirty-minutes ago. Grabbing my M4, I ran out of my CHU and hustled to the bunker. Half-dressed soldiers scrambled around, trying to find shelter.

The ground reverberated with continual attacks, each impact vibrating through my body. We huddled in the bunker. The fight between sleep and duty raged within me.

"All clear, all clear, all clear!" resounded through the base loudspeaker.

Exhaustion creeping in, I hustled to my squad's rally point. With all my soldiers accounted for, my platoon sergeant gave me the privilege of returning my body to its oasis. My pillow cradled my head, and I slipped back into dreamland.

"Ugh," I groaned at the blaring alarm. I looked over to see my roommate still asleep. "Flores, get your lazy ass up!"

"Two more minutes."

"There is no such thing as two more minutes with you. Get. Up!"

I needed coffee ASAP. Dragging myself out of bed, I threw on my Army Combat Uniform, (ACU) and walked over to my roommate.

"Get up, lazy bones." Irritated, I gave her a not so gentle shake.

"I'm up, I'm up." Flores arose.

After ensuring my roommate was not going back to sleep, I headed to the bathroom CHU next-door. I came back to the room to find my roommate still rifling through her drawer for clothes.

"I'll meet you at the Motor pool. I need to check the Communication and Warlock system's before the platoons rollout."

"Don't forget to start the coffee when you get there," she yelled.

"I would never forget such a mission-critical item." I closed the door and raced to the office.

My routine had been set. Start the coffee, grab my tools then head to the trucks. The vehicles were always checked before they headed out on a mission. My fear was always that the communications equipment would fail if I didn't check them before they went out. They're like my babies, and I needed to make sure they were okay before they set off on their own. It never failed that at least one system didn't want to cooperate.

The sun rose and all the trucks' Communications and Warlock systems were up and running. Finally. With the military police platoon trickling in to do their pre-mission checks, I dashed out of the motor pool to the Alpha company compound. Their trucks needed checking before their route clearance mission.

It was a two-mile trek from the Battalion Motor pool to the Alpha Company compound. When I trudged in, I diverted my eyes from the Commander talking to Sergeant First Class (SFC) Stacey. Hopefully, he did not see me.

"Specialist Davis," yelled CPT Briggs, the Alpha Company Commander.

Shit!

"Yes, Sir." Hustling over to the commander, I stopped in front of him and snapped to attention.

"At ease," CPT Briggs said with a wave of his hand. "The

Battalion Command Sergeant Major cleared you to go on a mission with the route clearance team to check the frequencies in the area."

"Roger, Sir. Do we know when that will be?"

"Sergeant First Class Stacey's team is preparing for a mission now. You will go with them."

"Roger, Sir. I need to get my gear."

"Jackson," CPT Briggs yelled to the soldier making his way towards the trucks.

"Yes, Sir."

"Take Specialist Davis to get her gear. It will be quicker if he drives you."

"Yes, Sir."

"Meet up with the route clearance squad at the back truck for the mission brief when done."

"Yes, Sir."

The team entered the compound. Returning with my gear I hustled to the trucks. They started their pre-mission checks while I checked their equipment.

"This morning we are clearing the route for the MPs detainee mission." SFC Stacey stood by his truck as he briefed us. "The MPs are releasing three detainee's in the city and we are going to clear their route of IEDs. Once the routes cleared, we are going to stop and let Specialist Davis," he pointed to me, and all eyes diverted to me, "out to take readings in the area where we have noticed cellular service on our routes. There will be a four-man escort team on Specialist Davis and the four gun trucks will position themselves at the four corners surrounding the road's intersection. Any questions?"

"No," the words rang out, in unison.

"Alright, load up," SFC Stacey yelled to the gaggle. "Specialist Davis, you will ride in the Buffalo."

Yay me!

I hated the Buffalo. It's a big behemoth of a vehicle with a huge robotic arm designed to dig up IEDs from the road.

The mission progressed smoothly. We drove down the MPs' planned route, clearing the road of any possible IEDs. With the route cleared, we drove to a known area that had cellular signal even with the trucks' warlock system on.

Of course, there was a signal. *We are so behind on upgrades.* Jackson and I climbed down from the Buffalo. Walking toward the center of the road I took snapshots of all the readings in different positions of the road.

The ground rumbled.

We hit the dirt, face buried in the sand as the area quaked from the disturbance. The impact was close. I scanned the skyline. To the east, was a cloud of smoke.

"Specialist Davis. Let's move!" said Jackson.

My escort rushed me to the vehicle in time to hear the Operation Center radio in, "the MPs got hit."

"What the hell?" I said, safely within the Buffalo. "We just cleared that route."

"That's the problem with route clearance," Jackson said, plopping into the seat next to me. He struggled to buckle himself in. "Sometimes they wait around for us to clear a route and set up an attack as soon as we leave."

"We are not that far from them so we will head their way to help." SFC Stacey radioed in. "Everyone saddle up."

We raced down the road, the Buffalo close to flipping over on the turns. When we reached the MPs, I wanted to cry, but there was no time to panic. The middle HUMMV was ablaze. SFC Stacey ordered me to stay in the vehicle. Although all soldiers trained for combat, support soldiers like myself were kept away from engagements. Chaos ensued as rounds sounded from both sides of the road. Soldiers scrambled like ants under a microscope to get the burning vehicle doors opened while others laid down suppressive fire. Sitting in the truck, I listened to the whole thing on the radio.

I have to help.

I scaled out of the Buffalo and joined the team laying down rounds to the left. Dropping to the ground, I sent rounds flying in three-round bursts.

SFC Stacey's order echoed in my earpiece, "Get in formation."

We moved as one force and pushed forward to clear the left side of the road. The team to the right did the same. I broke ranks and ran left of the formation.

I raced in a crouch position 500 meters and advanced. The soldier on my right did the same on the opposite side, leaving the insurgents trapped as we converged upon them. Approaching the two insurgents, weapon raised, I prepared to take my shot. There was a crack in the air. The insurgent's body dropped. His partner, stunned and now surrounded, dropped his AK-47 and raised his hands above his head.

We dragged the detainee back to the truck. I shot a glance at the truck on fire. Flames remained, but they were minimal. It was a miracle the soldiers got out. The HUMMV melted. The vehicle had been flattened to about three inches off the ground.

We hooked it up to the Buffalo. With MPs in tow, we raced down the dusty roads kicking up the stench embedded in the earth. We neared the entrance to the base. SFC Stacey called in our estimated arrival time to the Command Center.

Pulling into the motor pool, I noticed an area sectioned off with tarps. Usually, it's just a slab of concrete with a metal frame built on it, but today they had secured tarps all around the frame. The Motor pool was eerily empty, except for the Senior Motor Sergeant, SFC Daniels, and the Chief, CW4 Murphy.

SFC Stacey announced over the radio, "Stay in the vehicles—break—Specialist Davis follow me to the tarp area—over."

I descended the back stairs of the Buffalo. After the firefight, my body ached from the weight of my gear. *Why did*

I have to meet with SFC Stacey? Why was there a tarp up?

"Specialist Davis," CW4 Murphy called out walking to the sectioned off area. "Once the wreckage is secured in this area, pull all the communications equipment from the truck."

"Yes, Chief."

SFC Stacey and Chief guided the truck into the tarp area. A million questions ran through my head but I knew better than to interrupt while they were coordinating actions like pieces on a chessboard. I stood by the tarp waiting for the truck to be placed in hiding when my roommate walked up.

"Action-packed day, huh?" Flores said, standing to the right of me.

"You could say that."

"Are you okay?"

"Yeah." I faced her. "It was all a little crazy."

"Did they tell you why the tarp is up?"

"No. Do you know?"

"Yeah, they don't want the other soldiers seeing the wreckage. Especially the newbies."

"I guess that makes sense. I'm glad they made it out of the truck."

"Let's go get some coffee and drop your gear. You're going to want to compose yourself before you pull the equipment."

"Okay." We walked over to the motor pool office. "What am I supposed to do after I pull the equipment?"

"Set them aside for now. The most important thing is to get the serial numbers to match with your master list, for accountability." Flores poured me a cup.

Coffee in hand, I drowned it in cream and sugar. After a couple of much-needed sips, I unbuckled my gear and dropped it. My gear hit the ground with a thud.

We were safe, for now.

Terry Hojnacki

Terry Hojnacki is an award-winning flash fiction author, editor, novelist, children's writer, poet, and lover of words. Her current works-in-progress include a children's picture book series and a middle grade adventure.

She is a member of the Detroit Working Writers, the Society of Children's Book Writers and Illustrators, Rochester Writers, the Shelby Writers Group, founder of the Tuesday Morning Writers, and facilitator of the Creative Writers Workshop.

When not lost in her own words, she edits manuscripts, reads, and encourages other writers to improve and promote their work.

Visit TerryHojnacki.com.

The Note

Terry Hojnacki

The blue glow of the television flickered eerily in the dark. Curled up on the floor in the corner of the room was a young boy. He kept his head tucked into his chest and his back to the other occupants. His faded Redskins t-shirt camouflaged him with the motel carpeting. His face hidden. His body tense. The boy closed his eyes and listened.

The reporter on TV droned on about terrorists in the Middle East, a fundraiser for a family who lost a loved one in a house fire, and school closings due to the extreme cold temperatures. Flashing red lights glared like an emergency signal from the screen as a breaking news story aired.

"Local police are investigating a plea for help left in an area restaurant," the reporter said. "Concerned wait staff called police when they found the note written on a napkin. Video from the restaurant security cameras show a young boy leaving the napkin note on the counter by the cash register. If you can identify this boy or the women he was with, please contact the police."

The heavy woman sitting on the edge of the bed screamed, "What the hell were you thinking?"

The boy coiled tighter.

From behind the closed bathroom door, the younger woman said, "Ma, what are you talking about?"

"The little shit left a note at the restaurant."

The door flew open illuminating the room in bright, white light. "He did what!" screeched the woman still holding a towel to her head.

"It's all over the news. The kid left a note asking for help."

"What else did they say?"

"They showed a video from the restaurant. You can see the little shit at the counter writing on a napkin." She paused. "And then they showed me paying at the register."

The younger woman kneeled beside her son.

"I wanna go home," he whined.

"I know, baby," she said, rubbing his back, "but ever since your Daddy got home from Iraq, he's not the same man."

"He could be!"

"No, he can't. Is that why you left that note? For Dad?"

"It was a joke," the boy mumbled.

Dropping the towel to her shoulders, revealing her new hair color, she said, "This is no joke. We have to leave. He knows where to look for us now."

Changing Times

Terry Hojnacki

The paint has chipped.
The pipes have dripped.
The paper is falling off the wall.
There are wrinkles in the carpet
Scratches on the floor
Hand prints chasing fingerprints in the upstairs hall.
The ceiling has a hole in it
where Dad was looking for a clue.
He was trying to find the bathtub leak when
he put his finger through.
Though the house is overcrowded
and the windows need repair,
We all know that something special
lives inside of there.
It's not something to put a finger on,
Nor touch up with a spot of glue.
No patch, no paint,
no nail or tacks,
not anything that's new.
What lives inside this special place
Has been growing through the years.
The house is filled with memories,
happiness and tears.
The love that's shared from day to day,
as we help each other grow,
Will see us through the changing times
wherever we may go.

Carolyn and Jake

Terry Hojnacki

Carolyn nibbled the rye crust of the half-eaten Reuben listening to Jake devour his share of the food they'd scrounged. She hated loud eaters. The lip smacking, wide-open mouth crunching, and worst of all, that slurpy, sucky sound as the food mixed with the saliva right before the eater inhaled it down their throat.

She cringed, holding back her gag reflex. "Can't you eat any quieter?"

Jake ignored her. He focused on the food. Just like every guy she'd ever known, don't distract him from filling his stomach.

Her tummy whined as she rotated the sandwich in her hands. They didn't look like her hands. Her hands were always satiny smooth with perfectly polished nails. These hands, covered in street grime, sporting chipped nails and cracked skin, couldn't be hers. She prided herself in her beautiful hands. She took a bite of the sandwich.

The cook at O'Malley's felt sorry for her tonight. While Jake rummaged for garbage leftovers, Carolyn had stopped to take in the smells of the Irish pub. She leaned against the brick wall, next to the open back door and breathed in deep. Oh, the smells. Fresh baked rye bread, sauerkraut, and, of course, the succulent, fall-apart-with-a-fork corned beef. She closed her eyes and imagined that first bite. When she opened them, the cook stood a few feet away holding a plate of unfinished food over the trash can.

He paused.

She glanced from him to the toppled corned beef and rye at the edge of the plate.

He offered her the leftovers.

Carolyn hesitated. Then, with her pinky out, she took the sandwich, whispered a thank you, and gracefully strolled down the alley to catch up to Jake.

Amidst crushed boxes and tossed to-the-curb litter, Carolyn sat and finished eating. "Time to move on," she thought. Soon the druggies would take over the alley looking to satisfy their pot-munchies, and she wanted nothing to do with that crowd.

Carolyn and Jake avoided contact with anyone as much as possible. Staying in the shadows, keeping quiet, and blending in with the background were all survival tricks. By Carolyn's recollection, it kept her free.

Tonight they'd sleep under the wooden handicap ramp of St. Josaphat's. Jake had found a way for them to crawl into the two-foot high space that was large enough for them to rest side by side. She covered the cement with today's newspaper, rolling an extra one for her pillow. Jake lay on his side, pushing his back as close to her as he could get. She stared at the stars through the openings between the floorboards, drifted off to sleep and dreamt of Ireland.

Sirens pierced the city din, startling Carolyn out of her already restless sleep. She remembered where they hid, rolled over, and pressed her tummy against Jake's back. Draping her arm over him, she closed her eyes. His warmth against her body reassured her.

Rays of morning sunshine peeked through the ramp. Carolyn curled her wrinkled hands into fists and rubbed the sleep dust from her eyes. Jake had wandered off. He was smart, but she worried whenever they separated.

Leaning on her elbow, she opened her pillow sack and rummaged for a snack. She found a cellophane bag of smashed soup crackers. Carolyn licked her finger and dipped it into the salty crumbs. She grinned at her coated fingertip, and plunged it into her mouth, the overly salted flavor shocking her morning taste buds. The cellophane crinkled as she dove in for more, savoring each finger of crumbs while waiting for Jake to return.

Loud footsteps approached her hideaway. Carolyn hugged her pillow sack and curled her body into a ball. If they weren't looking for her, they'd never notice her here.

The ramp rained dirt, onto Carolyn, as heavy feet walked over her. Tiny hurried footsteps followed.

"Daddy, is Grandmamma here?" asked a tender, young voice.

"We hope so, Carrie. We hope so."

"Grandmamma! Grandmamma!" called the child as she stopped above Carolyn. "Where could she be, Daddy?"

Carolyn looked up between the slats at her granddaughter's tennis shoes. They were so close. Her namesake, dressed all in pink, came to find her. Carolyn pressed her fingers against her temples. If only she could be with them, but they wanted to make her sell her house, and leave Jake. Then, they planned to lock her up in a nursing home. *Please Jake, don't come back till they're gone.*

Her son answered little Carrie. "Father Roman said someone saw an old woman near the church. We're hoping they saw Grandmamma and Jake."

"Jake is with Grandmamma!" Carrie squealed.

"Sweetie, we're not sure."

"But Daddy, would Grandmamma go anywhere without Jake?"

"I don't know, but we'll find them," her son said, taking Carrie's hand as they strode down the ramp. "I want to invite Grandmamma and Jake to live with us."

Carolyn lay still. He'd invited her in the past. Then his wife found out what he planned, and *She* took Carolyn to the nursing home. *She* told everyone that Carolyn was crazy. *She* left Jake alone. *She* was a witch with a capital "B."

Their voices grew quieter. They were going away when Jake belly crawled under the ramp. Carolyn wrapped her arms around him, laid her head against his shoulder, and cried. She swallowed her cry when little quick steps ran up the ramp again.

"Daddy, I saw him! Really!"

Jake squirmed out of Carolyn's hug and barked. Carolyn grabbed for his collar, but it was too late. Her granddaughter peeked into their hiding place.

"Grandmamma, we found you!"

ABOUT

Sterling Script: A Local Author Collection

Like us on Facebook at
https://www.facebook.com/LocalAuthorCollection

Would you like your flash fiction, short stories, poetry, or
creative nonfiction considered for publication
in our next volume?
Email **localauthorcollection@gmail.com**
to be placed on our mailing list.

Submission dates and guidelines for the
2019 edition of Sterling Script
COMING SOON.